201

Surviving to Thriving

Jesaiah's Love

201

...

Surviving to Thriving

DEMETRIS MOORE HANEY

Copyright © 2021 by Demetris Moore Haney

All rights reserved.

Publisher's Notes

This book or any part thereof may not be reproduced or used in any manner without the express written permission of the publisher, except for the use of brief quotations in a book review.

Limits of Liability and Disclaimer of Warranty

This book is strictly for informational and educational purposes. It is used to educate and entertain. The author does not guarantee that anyone following these techniques, suggestions, tips, ideas, or strategies will become successful. The author and publisher shall not be liable for your misuse of this material. The author and/or publisher shall have neither liability nor responsibility to anyone with respect to any loss or damage caused, or alleged to be caused, directly or indirectly by the information contained in this book.

ISBN: 9798764713854

Scriptures in this book are from the King James Version (KJV) Bible, in the public domain, and the Holy Bible, New International Version®, NIV®. Copyright© 1973, 1978, 1984, 2011 by Biblica, Inc.® Used by permission. All rights reserved.

Bishop's sermon titles: mtzionnashville.org
Tasha Cobbs' song title: "Fill Me Up/Overflow"
Tamela Mann's song title: "I Can Only Imagine"
LaShun Pace's song title: "There's a Leak in This Old Building"

Published by Demetris Moore Haney. For information on the content of this book, please email Jesaiahslove@gmail.com

Printed in the United States of America

Dedication

Jesaiah's Love is dedicated to my loving husband, 201, family, friends, and everyone on this journey of surviving to thriving.

While experiencing immense pain, God's grace and mercy filled me with a special type of love created to ease hurt. When surrounded by unhappiness, it is important to find comfort and peace in loving oneself while accepting healthy love from others. If you remain humble and grateful when encountering a love as Jesaiah's Love, you will forever be changed.

A special thanks to all those who continuously believed in me, prayed when I never knew you were praying, and provided encouragement when I wanted to give up. As I know now, it is bigger than me along this path of surviving to thriving! You will forever hold a special place in my heart.

Contents

Dedication	
Preface	i
Chapter 1	
Surviving	1
Chapter 2	
Family Love	5
Chapter 3	
Those Three Words	11
Chapter 4	
Mind, Body, Spirit	17
Chapter 5	
Resilience	22
Chapter 6	
There You Are	37
Chapter 7	
Philippians 4:13	50
Chapter 8	
Life with Exceptional Testimonies	60
Chapter 9	
Thriving	78
Chapter 10	
Missing You	88
Epilogue	108
Acknowledgments	110

Preface

May 14, 2018, at 3:43 pm

AS I SIT IN THE AIRPORT AND WAIT ON A FLIGHT TO DEPART, I start to reflect on my visit to Jacksonville, Florida. My husband, Jai, and I had been planning this trip since last year to TPC. My "sister4life," Tonya, received tickets and reached out to him about attending. A few months before the flight, I experienced severe headaches and had to receive extensive scans. All the results were mainly clear, but I was informed of having syncope, vertigo, and migraines. I had been taking medicine and doing seemingly well. However, two days before takeoff, I had a major sickle cell crisis that caused pain in my tailbone and leg. It was a mild crisis, and I thought I could manage with a little pain medicine.

Within hours, the pain escalated, resulting in my inability to get out of bed without help. I knew if I went to the emergency room, they would admit me, so I pushed through the pain and called my hematologist the following day. It was not looking well, so I also called my mom to see if she could stay with me. I wanted to take precautions in case I had to be admitted into the hospital and could not talk my way out of it.

My only shot at staying hospital-free was going to my hematologist-oncologist for fluids and medicine the day before our scheduled flight to Florida. I was in severe pain and could barely walk. When I went to the restroom, Jai had to assist me with getting out of bed and walking. My body was giving me all the signs of not being able to go on our trip, but I wanted my husband to experience seeing Tiger Woods play in person. He was quick to let me know that if I was too sick and unable to travel, he was not going, period.

I eventually went to the doctor. The nurse drew blood samples and started an IV to give me some fluids and medication. My body was still in pain. The hematologist informed me that the crisis in my tailbone was affecting my leg and ability to walk. I explained we had a trip planned for the next day. She administered more medicine and I drifted off to sleep. I woke up and was able to stand. My hematologist made it clear that I should follow up with her or go to the ER if my symptoms did not improve. I felt better in the moment, and I knew if I continued to feel better, I was going on the trip. The next morning, I was able to walk without assistance. "I'm going." I soon learned the real reason that I pushed forward and was able to go to Florida.

We went to the airport early to make sure I would have time to walk without rushing. Our flight departed, and we arrived safely. We had a great time. I took it easy and tried not to overdo it while we ate, shopped, and engaged in memorable conversations. It was a blessing to spend time with loved ones and witness some of God's amazing plans. On that Sunday, Mother's Day, Tonya received a text from one of her friends that she wanted me to meet. Atiya came over later that evening, and what a blessing it was to meet her. Tonya was right. We had a lot in common as we began to share our testimonies. We talked, laughed, and I shed tears of sadness in preparation for a massive revelation.

The next morning, I thanked God for the opportunity to have met Atiya and started replaying our conversation in my head. I said Lord, maybe, I should include 33 in the book's title because that was the age when I thought I would die just as my brother had. Plus, I was diagnosed with breast cancer three weeks after turning thirty-three, and Saiah became ill three weeks after I finished chemotherapy and radiation. I continued to think about it and said God, I really want Jesaiah's Love in the title. Remembering, God says to ask in His name, and it will be given. As I stood in the bathroom, leaning over the sink with the water running, thoughts began to consume me. I wondered, should I tell Tonya about the winding circle, heart, and other symbols I drew on the shower glass every morning? How I dropped the number 8 off of 2018 when I came to the heartbreaking realization that I was unable to publish the book by Jesaiah's birthday in 2018?" I concluded, she would read about it when the book is released. Then God showed me Jesaiah's Love 201.

I asked God, "Like a college 101 course?" He said yes. I began to see Jesaiah's Love 201, 201.5, 301. God revealed, "Because it's bigger than you!" Complete generational overflow! I started to think about Bishop and how he told us that this year would be bigger than last year. Tasha Cobbs' song began playing in my head, "I'm getting ready to see, something I've never seen. God's about to blow my mind! It's bigger than I can imagine!" I cried out immensely and thanked God for generational blessings because I knew it was bigger than me! God said, "You did not publish Jesaiah's Love by his birthday in 2018 because it's bigger!" I thanked Him and realized why the song "Fill Me Up/Overflow" came to mind after my morning prayer. He was about to run me over for others.

I had been writing "JLove 201" on the shower glass every day for the past five months and thought it was due to knowing I would not get the book published in 2018. God had already worked the title out and was waiting on me to see what was directly in front of me. I have learned that He positions certain things in front of us, but we are unable to see them until we step out of our own way and see God's will. My way was 2018, but God's will was 201. I thank God for His will and not my way! God prepares us and gives us exactly what we need when we need it.

To experience Jesaiah's Love to the fullest, please take a moment to review the pictures and share the love with someone. As you read this, please open your heart and mind. I pray your heart will be filled with God's love to overcome some of your mind's most painful moments. Abundant blessings to you!

"AND NOW THESE THREE REMAIN - FAITH, HOPE, AND LOVE. BUT THE GREATEST OF THESE IS **LOVE**."

-I Corinthians 13:13 NIV

Chapter 1
Surviving

Foundation - God First

  TEARS ROLL DOWN MY FACE as I begin to experience one of life's most undesirable feelings. Pain! Some know this feeling as physical, mental, emotional, financial, and even spiritual pain. There are times when my life and pain seem to coexist. How could one person experience a life of pain and still remain? I ask myself this question several times as I sit amid white, balled-up tissues filled with insurmountable hurt and pain. Is this life? Is this how I am supposed to exist?

  My throat is consumed with aching knots of endless pain. I withhold from crying aloud as the sound of hurt is muffled with my hand cupped over my mouth. I want to cry aloud, but I hold the scream within. Tears flowing uncontrollably as the doctor looks down and says, "He could die from this." The pressure builds, and I try to hold it in but, no longer is it possible. A loud, painful cry is released. "Please help. What will I do?" How can I remain through this pain?

TODAY IS APRIL 12, 2014, and I have been encouraged to keep a journal throughout my journey. I was diagnosed with breast cancer on March 28, 2014. Three weeks after turning 33 years of age. Saddened? Yes... Shocked? Definitely. Was this a coincidence, test of faith, jinxing, or just another journey? You may ask, why would coincidence come to mind? I am the youngest out of five children, and my oldest brother and I are the two who were diagnosed with Sickle Cell Anemia and Cancer. My brother passed away at the age of 33, and I have always said I would do the same. Never did I think I would be diagnosed with cancer as well. Did I jinx myself, or did God allow me the opportunity to peek into my future? I guess we will find out at the end of this journey I call *life with exceptional testimonies.*

The past few weeks have been very emotional and painful as I come to grips with having breast surgery on **April 15, 2014, at 8 am.** This is one day before my son turns four years old, and I am concerned about celebrating his birthday after surgery. I want him to be happy on his special day as his birthday is unquestionably special.

The journey from April 2010. I was in Mississippi and had a major sickle cell crisis on Easter Sunday. I was extremely ill and had to be rushed to the hospital. The doctors did not know if the baby and I would make it. At 28 weeks, God allowed 1 lb. 10 ounces of an amazing angel into my life. I'm so grateful for my son, and I know *I must remain...even through this pain.*

Living through the process of cancer, I imagine being self-conscious of scars and saddened by hair loss. I wonder how others will react when they see me. I question how my son's father will respond with part of me missing and potentially no hair. I have pondering questions such as, *will he love me for better or for worse?* What will removing part of me change? To be honest, *will I love me for better or for worse?*

Transparently, during this journey, I may not love myself for better or worse. I can blame it on many factors, but it comes down to acknowledging that self-conscious, low self-esteem part of existence. I wonder how my life will change as I consider a lumpectomy, mastectomy, and even a double mastectomy. Whatever decision, I know my life will be altered forever as I receive encouraging words from my ministers, doctors, co-workers, friends, and family.

There are days when I smile, days when I cry, and days when I just try to remain. I realize that God always knew this would be a part of my life, and it is in His timing. Proverbs 2:8 (NIV) reminds me that "He guards the course of the just and protects the way of his faithful ones." I am grateful, and I pause to give Him thanks for protection. As my relationship grows with God, I know He will continue to prepare my heart, mind, and body for His will. I must trust and believe that it will be okay. Even as I ask, *Will I need breast reconstruction? Will I need mental reconstruction?* I know that He has the answers and knows what is best.

I try not to worry about the opinions of people, but sometimes I echo what others say, even if it is just a tiny amount for a minuscule timeframe. When perceiving something as negative, there is a tendency to allow negativity to engulf spirits. If I remain optimistic and in good spirits, it increases the likelihood that those around me will do the same. I must be strong for my son and continue to smile for him when I want to cry. I believe that everything happens for a reason; if this is my season to leave this place, I know that God will prepare me accordingly.

Chapter 2

Family Love

Family Next

I AM A 33-YEAR-OLD FEMALE who shocks people when I introduce myself as Demetris Moore Haney. Many assume I am a male until I speak with them, or they see me in person. God allowed my parents to create and raise me in the small town of Houlka, Mississippi. We did not have many expensive belongings growing up, but we were blessed with the necessities for endurance. We were surrounded by love from our parents, family, community, and our Heavenly Father. There were selfish moments when I did not feel loved due to not getting what I wanted or felt I needed at the time. I was the youngest out of five children, and I must admit, it certainly came with pros and cons. I did not have to personally encounter as many life lessons as my older siblings informed me of the *dos* and *don'ts*. Being the youngest also came with that sibling love of being manipulated out of my candy and money. I can recall, "I'll trade you three of my monies (COINS) for your one money (single bill)," which was not even close to the same amount. Sibling love. I soon learned to say, "I ain't got no money." I continued to make up for their trickery as "I ain't got no money" carried on as I grew older.

Loving each other and God was heavily instilled in our lives growing up. It was because of our strong foundation that we were able to sustain many storms in life. Storms arrived in several forms, but God and love kept us grounded. We had each other, and we still have each other today, with our oldest brother looking down from heaven.

My parents married at a young age, and they were genuinely in love. My mom lived with Auntie, and when my dad married her, Auntie told him to bring her back home if he did not want her. I can remember my mom having food prepared when my dad returned home from work. Initially, mom did not work much, but she made certain the house was cleaned and organized. Dad was the breadwinner, but he cleaned up as well. I was close to my parents, but I had typical childhood moments when they made me 'sick.' I never said this aloud (of course), but I would mumble it whenever I was told *no*. I tended to ask my dad for things versus my mother because he was likely to say yes without asking any questions. I am still close with my parents, and I strive to talk to them often.

Our parents made us go to church. We were on the usher board, sang in the choir, and my oldest brother was a deacon. We attended a small church not far from our home, and I remember having to catch a ride on some Sundays. Our parents provided for us and made sure we had food to eat and clothes to wear. We did not have a lot of money, but God always provided through His grace and mercy. We went to church, prayed, and believed in God throughout my childhood. There were a few options in our home but going to church and attending school were not two of them. Even as exhausted teenagers, if we were out late the previous night, we still had to attend church/school. It was a challenge standing properly to usher when you were sleep-deprived. It seemed as if the hymns were the exact same tempo and sleep was all around you, even the elders. We had a duty to serve, and we quickly learned accountability for our actions.

As a young child, Auntie was my Sunday school teacher, and she made certain we were attentive in her class. We had to read about Jesus and not laugh while others were reading aloud. If you made the mistake of laughing, you had to stand in the corner with your nose touching the wall. She also taught us to pay money in church and to always respect our elders. After church, we would want to play and run around outside of the building. If you ran past Auntie, she would stop you and say, "You gonna sang Sunday." You would instantaneously stop. As a little child, you did not want to sing in front of the entire church. That following Sunday, you were hoping she forgot, but it never failed. Auntie would tell you to stand up and sing. The accountability was consistent from home to church.

I did not have an opportunity to know my maternal grandparents, but I interacted with my paternal grandparents. They lived nearby, and we would go to their home often. As a kid, I always thought my grandfather was so nice and my grandmother was mean. Of course, our perception plays a major role in how we feel we are treated by others. I can remember asking my grandfather for some of his cinnamon roll. He would pinch off an extremely small piece and give it to me. I would laugh and take it, then he would always give me another piece of it or say, "Go in there and look on the table and get you one."

His freeheartedness reminded me a lot of my father, who made me share as well. My grandmother did not share as much, and she frequently would say no. I quickly learned to just ask my grandfather. He was an incredibly special man who called me "Pretty Bo-Bo." We would read bible verses and sing gospel songs at times. He walked often and would wave at every car that passed by. When I was in high school, people would ask, "Is that your grandfather who waves all the time?" I would tell them, yes, that's BoBo. They are both deceased now but will always be remembered in our hearts.

My maternal grandparents passed away when I was a child, but my mother was raised by my great Aunt (Auntie) and Uncle (Bill). Uncle Bill was an exceptionally quiet man. He passed away when I was a young adult. Auntie was born in 1922 and she was a hoot! My grandfather would say we did not stand a chance with our genes from Ida Mae (maternal great Aunt) and Earie Mae (paternal grandmother).

Auntie was the oldest mother of the church and overly direct most days. I would stay with her when I was a child, and she made the fluffiest biscuits ever! When I was in high school, Auntie made me a small pan of six biscuits. I ate them all with just jelly. I tried to get her to make some a few years ago, but she said, "I just don't have it anymore." You could be talking, and during a conversation, she would say, "You just getting so fat." We told her several times not to say that to people because you never know what someone is going through. She continued to say it but ended it with, "Oh yeah, they told me not to say that." She passed away in 2018, at the age of 96.

Lee was my oldest brother, and he was raised by Auntie and Uncle Bill. He set the stage for us at school for being the very precocious child that he was. Lee did not play often, and when it came to intelligence, he defined it. He graduated top of his class, and he received a doctorate degree at the age of 33. He was a math instructor and traveled the world as a missionary.

Lee was the one person who I knew would let me know when I was doing something wrong. If I were going to a party and he knew I had finals, he would tell me, you know you should be getting rest or studying for your finals. He did not believe in wasting time and wanted you to make the most of the opportunities presented to you. He pushed me to be better and always reminded me to not give up. He was and still remains my greatest inspiration. I am forever grateful for God allowing my brother to grace us with his presence for those amazing years.

We were taught to "treat others as you would like to be treated and to love your neighbors as you love yourself." I did not understand why I had to be nice to people who were not nice to me. I wanted to be treated kindly, and maybe, those who were unkind to me desired the same in some areas of their life. It was challenging to treat others the way I wanted to be treated when I was not the recipient of thoughtfulness. The process of maturity granted me the ability to spread kindness when I wanted to do otherwise.

Sometimes we struggle with knowing how to give love because of personal experiences. I pondered how is it possible to love your neighbors when you do not love yourself? What are the consequences when you are unable to love yourself? When you have not received healthy love, it is challenging to accept and bestow unconditional love. Often, the way we have received love is our perception of how love should be. At times, subconsciously. When it is unhealthy love, it can affect our ability to give proper love. We must try to make a conscious decision to end the harmful cycle. It is imperative to love oneself while taking care of your heart. This helps to increase the likelihood of a healthy heart, mind, body, and soul. While being vigilant about what is shaping your heart, strive to treat yourself with kindness and unconditional love. When loving God and ourselves, we can increase our thoughtfulness to others. My foundation is God, family, and love. Without God, I would not have family; I would not know healthy love without God and family.

My family did not constantly do everything right, and we never will. We certainly did not always agree, but we came together with God and love. There are times today when I think about my family and smile, as I am grateful. He allowed me to be a part of such a loving family unit. Even though I received love, loving myself was not always easy. I had to love myself when I did not feel loved, smile at mistakes while learning from them, and be kind towards myself to extend compassion to others. I learned to pray when I wanted to yell, forgive when I wanted to hold grudges, and celebrate the time in life that has been given to me. My foundation taught me to *love, smile, and be kind to one another. Pray, forgive, and celebrate life.*

Chapter 3

Those Three Words

You Have Cancer!

IT IS APRIL 16, 2014, and I had my surgery yesterday. The surgery went well, but I am in a bit of pain today. They removed some lymph nodes to test for cancer, and I should receive the results in a few days. My amazing sister (Shelia) and aunt (Pearlene) arrived yesterday morning around 4:30 am. I did not tell my sister the surgery had been pushed back to 8 am from 6 am. Jai told her she was on time. The four of us went to the hospital and made it back yesterday around 4 pm. My outstanding sister (Pam) arrived last night around 11 pm. I am so blessed by my family and support system. I thank God for surrounding me with astounding people.

Speaking of fantastic, today is Jesaiah's 4th birthday! He is such a joy who I love more than words can express. Four years ago, was a rough time and we are thankful to celebrate his life today. He makes me smile as I receive the best hugs in the world. I am unable to hold him, but he continues to give those Jesaiah hugs and kisses. This will be a journey for us all. I pray that God directs us as we step out in faith and go through this season. I strive to take it one day at a time while remembering to release my worries and concerns to Christ.

As I think back, I was lying in bed and felt a lump in my left breast. I went to my OBGYN doctor, and she sent me for an ultrasound that same afternoon. After completing the ultrasound, the radiologist explained I needed a mammogram due to the results. I thought to myself, I am only 33, and I need a mammogram. Upon completion, he contacted my OB doctor, who requested I call her after the appointment. I called her, and she proceeded to say that they had scheduled a biopsy for the following day. I knew instantly, it was not good. Jai and I arrived at the Breast Specialist to have the biopsy completed. She completed the biopsy and indicated she would take it down to the pathologist for review herself. Within an hour, the Breast Specialist called us into her conference room. She walked in, shook her head, and said those dreadful words, "You have breast cancer."

As she continued to talk, tears filled my eyes and rolled down my face. It was as if I knew, but I did not know. Jai and I had discussed the likelihood of cancer due to the rapid actions and the Breast Specialist walking my test to another doctor in the adjacent building. She provided us with an abundance of material and said she wanted to treat it immediately and aggressively. I only remember portions of what she explained. My thoughts entered a mental space, and I continued to repeat internally, "I have breast cancer." I think I was trying to convince myself that I had breast cancer at the age of 33. The more I thought about it, the more sadness and anger started to intertwine, and those feelings were building up… "I cannot believe that I have breast cancer!"

Jai and I walked out of her office and looked at each other. We hugged and did not have to say anything as we both were consumed with internal thoughts and feelings. We went by my office so that I could grab some work material and went home. We barely communicated during the drive. I think we both silently understood each other's needs at the time. It was a Friday afternoon, and I knew all my family was at work. I decided to call and tell them personally as I sat on the end of the bed looking out of the window.

I called my mom, who lives in Mississippi first, and she did not answer. I proceeded to call my father, and he did not answer either. I knew then it was on to the siblings. I called my oldest sister, Pam, in Miami. I asked her how she was doing, and I went on to tell her that I had just left the doctor, and the doctor informed me that I had breast cancer. That was the first time saying it aloud to someone. It was very painful. We both cried as we tried to talk, but she said she would call me back. I called my brother and said, "Broham, I went to the doctor, and she said I have breast cancer."

I felt it was easier if I just came out with it at the beginning of the conversation. My brother cursed repeatedly and said he would call me back as well. I took that as if they both were gathering themselves to be able to talk to me. I think we all were very shocked and did not know what to say.

I continued with the phone calls as I needed to personally inform the family. I called my sister4life, Tonya, in Texas, but she was unable to answer. My sister, Shelia, was on a cruise with her husband, and I did not want to interfere with their vacation, although I wanted to be the one to tell her. I reconsidered and called anyway. As always, she was very encouraging. Shelia's words were positive and God-filled.

My brother called me back with my dad on the phone. Dad reassured me with, "We'll get through it."

My mom called soon after and told me she had spoken with my sister, Pam. I knew my family was aware and it would quickly spiral, so I sent Tonya a text message:

> "Hey girl! How are you! I was just calling my sisters; bro to tell u guys that I found out today that I have breast cancer. ☹ I will keep you posted. Love you lots!!!"

As tears rolled down my face, I realized even typing the words brought sorrow. Tonya replied:

> "Will call u tomorrow. Speechless and praying and crying. Love you so much. Do u want to talk now or too soon? I am here for you".

I had accomplished the painful goal of making sure they were aware before others heard the news. I wanted to ensure that they received accurate information directly from me. I trusted them with my fears, and they were strong enough to handle them in a supportive manner. I was getting ready to go through a storm that would affect my normal state of being. God had surrounded me with loving people to help with the potential harm I would face. All storms are capable of destruction. I did not want to be destroyed emotionally or physically, and I needed support from those I felt would undeniably be there without judgment.

I have learned that many people are supportive, but they bring judgment along with them. They start asking questions such as, "Do you think it's something you have been eating? What do you think you did to cause it?" I have never understood why we allow others to bring rain when we are already in a storm. I know that storms and rains can alleviate droughts, but I did not think I was experiencing a drought at the time. Maybe I was and did not know it. I could have lacked a necessity for growth. Would this be occurring to provide me with what I needed? Storms bring about change, and it is up to us to decide if we will use that change to generate positivity or pessimism.

I was informed by quite a few people to "just hand it over to God!" Handing it over is very appealing and is a lot easier said than done when going through trials. There have been several times in my life when I "thought" I handed it over to God. The challenge that I encounter is not saying it but turning it completely over to God. Like many, I have said yes, I am giving it to God, for there is nothing too hard for Him. I "give" it to him, and then I find myself still playing tug a war as I try to deal with it. I found myself kneeling and praying, asking God for deliverance but would then stand and still have thoughts of concern. I questioned, does that come from a lack of trust in God? But he's God! How could I not have faith in him? It was a feeling as if I had to deal with life on my own and not wholly activating Matthew 11:28, where he informs us to "Come to me, all who labor and are heavy laden, and I will give you rest."

In life, we are often taught to be independent, and it can sometimes lead to not allowing others, including God, to help us in time of need. Ultimately, we must realize that our Heavenly Father can handle all our problems and needs. I trust and love Him dearly, so I told God that I was turning the diagnosis of cancer over to Him. I proclaimed it, and now my greatest challenge consists of letting it all go. Could I release all this sadness and hurt? Only time will tell as I strive to do my best.

I ask that He strengthens me to handle the situations to come while providing grace and mercy during this journey. I believe that God will not place more on me than I can withstand, and I must have faith. I have assurance, and I am blessed with the ability to share the worry of bearing the effects of receiving chemotherapy with my support system. As God prepares me for His will, I realize changes will occur mentally, physically, spiritually, and emotionally. Thoughts start to emerge as I question being "prepared" to lose hair and experience nausea with weakness. Some may suggest wearing a wig and taking medicine, but does that mentally prepare you? Maybe physically, but truthfully, I do not feel ready to go through this storm. The more I think about it, the more worry builds. The process is going to happen. It is not going to be easy, but doable with effort and commitment. My life is filled with distress because of worrying, crying, and trying to figure out God's plan for my life. Pondering, *Will I be okay?* I know that He will reveal it when the time is right, so I pray for peace and strength to help during this journey.

Chapter 4

Mind, Body, Spirit

Preparation

    ONE THING I HAVE NOTICED ABOUT GOD and storms is that He often gives me moments of revelation. They have occurred throughout my life. I think back on all the times I have experienced "revelations." Before something would happen, I would encounter signals of the outcome beforehand. I thought I was stopping myself, but God was covering me. He knew that I needed proof before acting. He has provided it extensively in my life, and I am starting to figure out why.

    When I was younger, I had a clear vision of having a wreck on a highway that I was unfamiliar with at the time. Afterwards, I did not think much of it. Years later, I was working in Knoxville, TN and had gotten lost on the same highway that was in my vision. Initially, I thought I was delusional, but then I started seeing the same signs. The road was exactly the same. As in the vision, I was approaching the point of wrecking. Anxiety was building. I said to myself, "Are you tripping or what? I have seen this before, but I have never been on this road." The revelation hit as I reached the point where I had wrecked in my vision. I stopped the car. My heart was pounding. I thought about it, turned around, and went back the other way.

This was not the only instance that occurred in my life. I was working on a school project with my nephew, Vell. While I was helping him, the vision came rushing back, revealing the exact project and him failing due to not completing it himself. In the vision, I remember him saying the teacher had given him a failing grade because he had not finished the project. When I was about to help my nephew with his school project, I stopped. I remembered the vision and told him he was capable of completing it. Another revelation consisted of writing a notice to my apartment complex about moving out. As I added the reason, I remembered the vision of not being able to move out for that particular explanation.

Some may say these are just instincts or common-sense occurrences. Earlier in life, I may have agreed, but I have learned that these were definitely more than intuitions and instincts. They were teachable moments. God's way of telling me to trust Him and to follow what He has already shown me. I could have continued down the same road where I had already seen myself wrecking. I could have completed the project with my nephew or added the reasoning to the letter. I chose not to because I had already seen the outcome. How many times have we already seen the outcomes but still chose to go down that path? There are times when I am guilty of this, and I ask God for guidance. The outcome of our decisions may be indirect. Still, we know the likely results of excessive drinking, unprotected sex, drug misuse, cheating, lying, theft, adultery, overeating, extreme stress, not exercising, gossiping, killing, hurtful words, smoking, fornication, and so much more.

These are only a few moments in which I had already anticipated the outcome with follow-through. Those were times in which I "knew" the end results, and I was able to deter them. For years, I said I would die at the age of 33 as my brother had. What about now? Was this destiny that I was diagnosed with breast cancer three weeks after turning 33 years of age? Did God allow me once again to peek into my future? Am I able to turn around or stop? These were consuming thoughts, and I had to trust God for guidance.

I believe everything occurs during a specific time and for a reason. Sometimes it feels as if things that happen are senseless, and other times, inevitable. If this is my season to leave this earth, I know that God will prepare us for His will. Will I be sad to leave all my loved ones? Of course, but I know God has already worked out what I am trying to work through. After I pray, a song by LaShun Pace, *There's a Leak in This Old Building*, repeatedly plays in my mind. The lyrics are,

> There's a leak in this old building, and my soul
> Has got to move
> My soul
> Has got to move
> Ooh, my soul
> Has got to move
> There's a leak in this old building, yo' and my soul
> Has got to move
> I've got another building
> A building not made by man's hands

When the song comes into my head, I automatically think that my time is up, and I will be leaving this place soon. I pray that God strengthens my family and friends and for them to realize that I will be okay. As this building leans and sinks, I know that God will either tear it down to rebuild or move it on to my eternal home. I thank God as He prepares us for His will and draws me nearer to Him. I know that God is preparing my heart, mind, and soul. I am so grateful for all that He does for my family and me.

I thank God for His love and for creating me in His image. It is such an honor knowing our heartbeats are in sync. God is preparing my heart by showing me love. Through His love and generosity, I can give love, smile, and enjoy life's moments even when I want to cry. There are times when I am sad and want to weep exceedingly. I can get through those moments because God loves me. He shows me this in so many ways (family sending me encouraging messages, friends bringing me funnel cakes, receiving gifts and cards right on time, and so much more love and support). I pray that I am a blessing to someone as He prepares my heart and walks with me. I tend to guard my heart, but when I open it to receive love, friendship, and kindness, I am apt to give the same.

The golden rule stands true, and when you put your whole heart into treating others the way you want to be treated, God extends grace and mercy towards you. I learned this many years ago. At first, God used me to receive love and kindness when I was not giving love and kindness as I should have. I took many things/people for granted, and I did not treat others the way I wanted to be treated. Then the roles were reversed, and I was giving love and kindness to others. I told myself that I received so much love and kindness and did not appreciate it as I should have. It was time for me to extend what God had blessed me with. I know it was only God as I was a very selfish person, and I did not like to share my love or "things." God placed me in a position to give my time, love, friendship, and kindness without receiving as I had before. This humbled me and allowed me the opportunity to be grateful for what God had given me to help others.

Chapter 5

Resilience

Process

MAY 9, 2014, AT 9:45 AM, the chemotherapy journey will begin. I ask myself, am I mentally prepared to receive chemo? I cannot say for certain, but I have prayed profusely, cried irrepressibly, and talked it over and over with loved ones. During one of my doctor visits, I was informed that I would receive a port due to extended chemotherapy treatments (sum of sixteen). Trying to grasp the fact of having an object placed in my body to receive therapy was particularly challenging. The questions started to arise ... What if something goes wrong? What if it causes other issues? Even though I questioned it, I knew it had to be done as I was a horrible stick and the thought of trying to start an IV on a regular basis was inconceivable. As I tried to prepare myself for the port, I began to think about outward appearances. I knew my hair was going to fall out as my oncologist said it would occur in approximately three weeks upon starting chemotherapy. I asked if this was just a possibility, and she explained that my hair would definitely come out because of the medicine. This concerned me, and I needed to figure out what I could do about it, if anything.

On May 3, 2014, I discussed my feelings and concerns openly with Jai, and he informed me that he would support me in every way that he could. I explained that I needed him to go with me as I ventured into the next journey. He undoubtedly agreed. As we got in the car, I began thinking about the process and how I would deal with everything. We drove about a mile to a large store in hopes of finding some help with my journey. I walked in and started looking around the store. It was immediately overwhelming. A female employee approached us and asked how she may help. I responded with, "I would like to try on some wigs." She asked if I was looking for a specific type, and I explained that I just needed one for everyday wear. She told me to look around, and she would get me a wig cap to put over my hair while I tried on the wigs.

There were several choices as we browsed through the selection. I wanted something of the norm. I picked out a few wigs, and Jai informed me that they all were remarkably similar as they were shoulder-length, black, and straight. That was normal for me, and he said he was going to pick one out. He selected a short one with golden highlights for me to try on. I thought this was not the norm. As I began to try the wigs on, reality hit in the sense that I was going to lose my hair. It was a little surreal as I pulled my hair back and placed it in a wig cap. The employee assisted with putting the wigs on and styling them. We discussed comfort and ways to style the various wigs. I decided to go outside of the norm and buy the short wig and a shoulder-length wig, too. I knew the wigs would help with the external appearance. I was unsure how they would help with the internal feelings of not having any hair.

Today is the day that I encounter what I feel will be my greatest challenge in this process... chemotherapy. As I prepare to receive treatment, I do not participate in my usual routine of spraying perfume after a shower. I was informed that perfumes may cause nausea, so I made sure not to wear anything scented. I walk into the doctor's office with my rock by my side. The lab technician calls me back to draw blood. She asks which side she may stick. I told her right as I had previously had a blood clot on my left side. She proceeds to draw blood from my right arm and directs me to the infusion room. She is explaining what is getting ready to happen, and I am attempting to process it all. As I walk through the doors, I see reclined chairs with patients from all backgrounds and genders covered in white blankets. Some are sitting up, while most are laying back as various fluids from IVs drip into their bodies. Some are with loved ones sitting in a chair beside them, and others without that much-needed support. The room is ice cold. It is filled with pillows, stools, chairs, magazines, water, snacks, and clinicians walking the floor. I hear the television softly playing in the background, and then I hear, "Pick a chair." The chair I wanted to pick was not in that room. I thought to myself, I would rather be at home in a chair.

As I wait on the nurse to arrive, I notice people around me sleeping, typing on computers, talking to loved ones, and listening to music. Jai and I are sitting there quietly, taking it all in. I see a nurse walking towards us. She pulls up a stool, says, "Hi, I'm Becky, and I will be your nurse for the day." She has a pile of papers and start going through them to describe the type of chemotherapy and other medicines I would receive during this process. Becky explains everything thoroughly, ensuring all our questions are answered before starting treatment. She tells me they were going to start my treatment and proceed to get her sterile packet. She comes back with gloves enclosed in a package and tools. She puts the gloves on and cleans the port that is on the right side of my chest. The medical team informs me of each medicine before starting it and say I would likely be able to taste some of it. I'm thinking *that's strange* and ask myself, *how would I be able to taste an IV fluid?* As they administer it, I quickly learn the answer to that.

During the process of receiving Cytoxan, the top of my head and nose started to burn. Initially, I did not mention the burning as it was mild, but the sensation increased dramatically. The nurse specified she would slow it down and run it over an hour during the next treatment to see if it would decrease the burning. After the first treatment was completed, I felt okay and did not experience much nausea or feelings of weakness. Becky said the steroids usually make you feel as if you can run a marathon on the day of treatment. I most certainly was not at the level of running but maybe a little brisk walking.

I was trying to do all I could to navigate through the entire process of having cancer. I often reminded myself that

"I have cancer; cancer does not have me!" I decided to continue working while setting my mind on other things. Realizing, working would keep me busy and focusing my mind on God will keep me in astonishing peace. I felt as if I had a plan and was slightly prepared for the process. I thought this was true until reality smacked me in the face on **Wednesday, May 21, 2014.**

    For the past few days, a burning sensation had been taking place on the top of my head as my hair was shedding. I recalled reading about this potential symptom. On this day, the burning had increased, and the shedding has progressed to coming out when rubbing my hair. I knew this day would come and I was prepared, right? I had read material on hair loss. Jai and I spoke about the process, and I informed him that I had been contemplating going to the hair salon to let them cut it before it all came out. Jai explained that he was willing to cut it for me if I was okay with it. I thought about it for a moment and told him that I did not want him to experience those emotions of cutting my hair. He assured me that he was willing to cut it and did not feel it would produce any negative emotions. I told him that I would think about it and let him know. I decided to reach out for a little extra support as I sent a picture of the excess hair shedding to my sisters. I told them I was thinking about getting it cut the following day after work because I did not want to wake up in a few days and see extreme hair loss in my bonnet or sink.

    I told a few friends and family members that I felt as if chemotherapy would be my greatest challenge in this process. I undoubtedly feared how I would look and feel during this treatment process. Questions arose, such as, *will I be nauseated constantly, will my appetite diminish, and will I lose weight?* So many more pondering thoughts. I knew that the experience was temporary, but I still worried about how I would feel and if the effects would impact me permanently. There were days when I tried to be strong and put on the "everything is well" face. I knew that I should not allow my fears to control my life, and I should not focus on them continuously.

It is great to have someone you trust and confide in. My only issue was trying not to worry or stress others with my own concerns and fears. I know how transference may occur when you are dealing with challenging situations. God places people in our lives to care for us and give us the support we need during seasons of growth. I believe we are equipped to handle what we encounter if we trust God, as He provides all the necessary tools we need to survive.

I have completed a couple of treatments, and I am starting to notice increased anxiety before chemotherapy. Every visit includes them drawing blood first and then going ahead with the treatment. However, the last visit did not go well. As usual, I arrived at the doctor's office, and they sent me back to have labs completed. Because I was in and out of the hospital over the last 30 years, I have developed a lot of scar tissue. I try to mentally prepare myself as I typically receive grief from technicians about being a hard stick. I can count the number of times I have only been stuck once to start an IV or draw blood. On the rare occasion that I encounter a nurse able to retrieve blood on the first stick, I ask if she is willing to accompany me to other doctor visits. Due to previously experiencing a blood clot and undergoing the removal of lymph nodes in my left arm, only my right arm can be used to draw blood.

I sat in the chair, and the nurse began searching for a vein. She said, "Your veins are small, and they roll." I told her yes, she was the lucky nurse today. She stuck me three times and was unsuccessful. On the third stick, she moved the needle around under my skin but still could not find the vein. She said she was not going to stick me again and went ahead to ask another nurse to try.

I started drinking water, and they covered me with a blanket. The second nurse tried, and she stuck me twice. By this time, I was beginning to get anxious. I tried to prepare myself for a few sticks, but if they are not successful by the 3rd or 4th, I start to get extremely nervous. They went to ask the oncologist if they could use the port, and she said no. They returned and placed warmers on my arm and hand. Another nurse stuck me in my hand, and then she stuck me in my arm. When she stuck me in my arm, she was able to get it on the 7th stick. I was tearful at this point, and she just kept apologizing for the multiple sticks. I told her it was not the worst, but it was up there.

I can remember going to the hospital to have a scan completed with contrast. It was supposed to take about 30-45 minutes. I was there for over three hours due to nearly having a panic attack after being stuck 11 times to complete a scan. The technician called for an ultrasound machine and a doctor to come and get the needle in my vein. He was not able to get it after 6 people and the 10th stick with the ultrasound machine. I was surrounded by 6 people who were not able to stick me. At this point, I completely lost it. Tears had been rolling down my face since around the 6th attempt, and I could no longer cry silently. I started crying aloud, and everyone left the room except the doctor. He apologized and asked me to sit on the table. He gave me some water, started talking about God and his family. I calmed down, and he said if he did not get it this time in my hand, they just would not be able to complete the scan today. He stuck me in my hand and got it on the 11th stick. But God!

After being stuck seven times, I headed into the treatment room. I sat in the chair, and the nurse tried to access my port. She was not able to get it after several attempts! I became so anxious she had to get the oncologist who discussed giving me some anxiety medicine to help calm me down. I told her I did not want to take more medication. She said I needed it to help with accessing the port as their inability to do so was causing me anxiety. I am sure many people think that it should be easy to receive medicine through a port, but if it is not aligned correctly, they must adjust it and will have you alter your body's position to gain access. I noticed that I become stressed when there are challenges with routine procedures after a certain time. I expect proficiency, but I have learned we all need grace and patience. There are moments when I have expectations and become anxious when they are unmet. Accessing my port was not getting better, so I started taking the anxiety medicine immediately before they attempted. I must admit, it helped to ease my stress during treatment.

I have been getting rest and trying to take naps during the day, so I don't burn out quickly. I noticed that during my normal daily routine, I must stop and take breaks. I cannot completely go through normal tasks (i.e., brushing my teeth, showering, doing my hair, etc.) that I could previously complete. I was informed to listen to my body, so I am trying to precisely do that. Well-balanced diet… hmmm honestly, not so much. I should be eating at least three meals per day and making healthy choices with limited sweets. The problem is…I do not have a good appetite, and my taste buds are horrible!

As I mentioned earlier, they have snacks and drinks in the treatment room for patients. I would periodically eat some of them; especially, the peanut butter crackers. I reached a point where I was just eating the crackers as I was unable to taste any flavor. I was told to eat healthy meals. I would usually try to eat something from Subway™ when I was receiving treatment because there was one downstairs. The smell would not be as loud as other foods. I would ask Jai to bring me a 6-inch turkey on wheat with American cheese, lettuce, pickles, and a little regular mustard. Initially, I would eat a few bites of the sandwich, but as time progressed, I did not eat much of it. My waning sense of taste and trying to eat while receiving treatment had a lot to do with not eating.

I stopped eating out as much and soon noticed the cost of food, gas, treatment, and household bills were continuously adding up. I started to think about the cost of having cancer and wondered if I had enough money to "complete it." I remember reading Luke 14:28 "Suppose one of you wants to build a tower. Won't you first sit down and estimate the cost to see if you have enough money to complete it?" Some may inquire how this verse is relevant, and I feel it is applicable not only through the process of cancer but along this journey called life, with exceptional testimonies. I have always been the person to plan things out and make a list to help with accomplishing goals. As I reviewed my finances and listed out bills, I knew expenses were adding up quickly. I spoke with a cancer advocate, and she informed me of several available resources for patients receiving treatment for cancer.

The process of receiving cancer treatment is expensive with or without insurance. I was employed full-time and had medical coverage during my treatment. I was grateful for having insurance, and I understood medical costs due to my numerous hospital stays. My finances were becoming very tight, and I had to budget everything. I can remember going into the dollar store (one of my favorite stores) and calculating that I was only able to buy five essential items. This was a huge challenge as I love buying numerous things there, but I recognized that I had limited funds and prioritized needs vs. wants.

As I continued to process everything, I chose to reach out to one of the available resources. I needed assistance. I waited until it was an absolute necessity as I did not want to receive resources that I did not need, and others did. My utility bill was due, and I was informed about a program to help with the payment. The cancer advocate provided me with all the information to send in for assistance. I reached out to the organization via email and included all the pertinent information. I received a blunt email response from the program assistant stating they were not going to pay my utility bill due to the timing. I knew that the information was submitted correctly and on time, but my mother always told me, "Metris, kindness will kill a person." I typed an initial response informing them it was submitted in the timeframe listed on their submission form with highlighted information and quotes. I thought about what my mom had told me, and I deleted the response and simply put, *Thank you for your hospitality* and *Have a blessed day*.

After sending the email, I said, "Lord, I hope that this will help her to be nicer to someone in the future." Within a couple of hours, I received the email response with the following words "I'll pay your utility bill." I knew that it was only by God's grace and mercy that she agreed to pay the bill. It made me think, how many times are we vindictive when we could be kind? I am not always kind, but I strive to treat others the way I would like to be treated. Many times, our responses are based on our environment. If we are around certain people, we respond a particular way. Most people are more respectful around their elders vs. peers. Through personal experience, I have learned to be respectful and, sometimes, just smile. I know that sincerity may be challenging when you are placed in a situation where you feel adaption is needed for acceptance. Remember to love yourself and God will never put you in a place where you cannot seek grace and mercy.

With the mindset of being in a positive environment, I decided to attend a "Look Good Feel Better" class. I was a little nervous because I didn't know what to expect. I was told that everyone in the class had cancer or had just finished the process. I wanted to attend the class to gain other perspectives and share my own experiences. When I walked in, the atmosphere was pleasant. Everyone was friendly. I noticed a room full of women of various backgrounds, ages, and ethnicities. It appeared to be an environment of acceptance. The feeling of knowing you are not the "only one" is like none other. Who wants to be alone in difficult situations? God knows where to place you, when, and the helpful people to surround you within those moments.

I often ask for guidance and discernment as I strive for sincerity. I met some remarkable women who shared their stories with me. I remember the introductions and thinking about how cancer does not discriminate. You never know when life's going to deal you a hand of sadness, hurt, pain, and discouragement. I met the first lady of a renowned church. She shared how she cut her hair after the first treatment due to it falling out in the front. We discussed how family and friends are such important assets during the journey. We were both young, black females, and our lives had taken a turn down a different road than expected. It was helpful to speak with other women and share experiences with laughter, tears, and acceptance.

There are several tools available to help get through the journey of cancer. Like many journeys in life, it is imperative to take the necessary steps to access them accordingly. For me, the greatest of all is the Word of God. When I wanted to give up and did not have the desire to push forward, I had to seek God for strength and direction. Was it always easy? Absolutely not. Through grace and mercy, I did not give up.

The American Cancer Society is another phenomenal resource. They connected me with other women who had endured cancer, and they called to check on me periodically. It was highly appreciated to have someone with similar experiences giving advice about concerns, struggles, and pain. Family and friends are a blessing, and I know their encouragement contributed to why I continue to push forward today. I am grateful as I realize the decisions that I make affect those who are around me. I have loved ones depending on me to make it through this season. I know that I will; while growing from the process through prayer, faith, and love.

It can be a challenge to start and keep a healthy lifestyle when you have made unhealthy choices for much of your life. It takes a lot of hard work and dedication to condition your mind and body. Stress impacts health tremendously and causes pain in many areas of your life. It is easy to say do not worry about things you cannot change, but it is not as easy to implement. I must make better choices by eating less sugar and carbohydrates while increasing exercise. As God makes choices about my life, I must do the same by trusting God, loving myself, and working toward a healthier lifestyle.

Giving up, letting go, and pressing forward. To ensure my progress during this journey, I must give up some of my unhealthy habits. My oncologist explained that there are some things I must change to increase the success of treatment. The first was on her list; I had to stop completely with chemotherapy. It was alcohol and wine. I must give it up until after completing my treatment. I must also stop drinking caffeinated beverages, decrease sugar intake, milk, and red meats. Whew…I knew it was going to be a challenge when she said restrict sugar intake.

This has always been a challenge for me since I was a young girl. Growing up, my father would bring me sweets home nearly every day after work. I love sugar then and still to this day. As I learned over the years, if I consume too much, it does not love me back in a healthy way. Why would I continue with a love that causes so many problems? It started during my childhood, and I made a choice to continue with it. I must decide to end it, or it will continue to affect me in many unpleasant ways. Life is full of choices, and we must be vigilant about what we carry from childhood into adulthood. Some of those things can be phenomenal, and others are harmful, even crippling.

I continue to tell myself, do better! Yoga, walking, Zumba, and cardio sounds very doable, but I have not started back doing any of the needed exercises. I should be taking better care of my health when it comes to eating and fitness, but I have chosen to sleep or just lay down instead. I need to start getting up and moving around as I know depression can quickly develop. I am more than capable of walking every week as it only takes a little time to start and establish a routine. I want to be healthy while living a long prosperous life, so I must decide to exercise for myself. Consistency is the key and habits are formed with repetition. If you want to achieve something, try doing it regularly.

I knew I had to start eating vegetables every week to achieve daily results and exercising a few minutes every day or every other day to get into the habit of doing it. God gives us abundant opportunities. It is up to us to seize the moments. I admit, there are moments when I miss opportunities due to not moving when God says move. I can lie on the sofa and watch television or stand up and do squats while watching television. I have placed my dumbbells by the sofa to use them while I am sitting. We must seize the moments that we have and make choices to do better, even if they are small ones.

"I can do all things through Christ which strengtheneth me."

-Philippians 4:13 KJV

Chapter 6

There You Are

Grateful

MOMMY TO REMAIN EVEN THROUGH THIS PAIN. What am I most thankful for? Some people see this question and think materialistic. I see this question and look at this precious brown-eyed, curly-haired, four-year-old blessing lying across the bed with me. I am most thankful for the blessing of family! I am grateful that God has allowed me to be surrounded by such loving, caring, and unselfish people. The amazing feeling of small arms wrapping around your neck, a kiss on the cheek, a hug with an extra squeeze, a text saying thinking of you, a card with 'you can do this,' and just asking what you need me to do.

When you are feeling down, seek God. He will show you how sometimes it is the small things that matter the most. It is a blessing to receive the love that makes you smile when you want to frown, laugh when you are almost crying, and express happiness when surrounded by sadness. When I want to give up and feel like I cannot move forward, I think about my loved ones and realize life is full of choices, but quitting is not one of them.

Romans 15:13 states, "May the God of hope fill you with all joy and peace as you trust in Him, so that you may overflow with hope by the power of the Holy Spirit." I asked myself, can I be joyful during this journey and overflow with hope? I trust God. I believe this journey is what I make of it. I know that having hope means I expect to get through this journey with the confidence that God has given me. His word tells me that He will fill me with joy and peace as I trust Him, but there were days when joy seemed so far away. Does this mean that I do not trust God? I think about the changes I am going through, and they are overwhelming. I pray and receive joy by believing things will get better. Every day is not great, but I know that life could be a lot harder if I did not trust God. There are moments when I am torn into pieces but striving to obtain peace. I have such immense joy when I look at Jesaiah and see him playing with cars, smiling, and celebrating life. As Jesaiah looks up at me and smiles, I smile with a warmth of overflowing hope. Trusting God to get through this process as he surrounds me with joy and peace from a smile of love.

I trust God as I move into phase II of the treatment process. Chemotherapy is scheduled twice weekly for three months and radiation daily for two months. I know it is only by God's grace and mercy that I will survive the experience. I have accepted the fact that I am going through chemotherapy, but I still have anxiety as they access my port weekly. It may be the fact of them sticking a needle in my chest! I feel the stress and worry increases, and I relate it to my previous experiences of being pricked an overabundance of times. I know that I will get through this as I take it one day at a time and even one moment at a time. Matthew 6:34 comes to mind as it tells us, "Therefore do not worry about tomorrow for tomorrow will worry about itself. Each day has enough trouble of its own." I have learned to live for today as we never know what tomorrow will bring. God allows me to inhale and exhale while enjoying the present moment. I am grateful for the ability to live in the moment.

Some may ask, how do I live in the moment? Is it easier to live in the past? I think we all answer these questions differently because we come from different walks of life. I believe we live in the moment by being present and accepting what is happening today. Acknowledging the now and embracing what occurs in the moment causes us to live in the present. Some people choose not to live in the moment because of having to be accountable and face the reality of what is occurring. What if we only knew of the current moment, and we were unable to remember our past or cognitively conceive what the future may hold? I feel many of us would experience life on a different level and enjoy living for the moment. We are given the precious gift of today, and we must be thankful as we consider all things. I try to enjoy every moment of the day and not take a second for granted. Smile, love, and be kind to one another. Pray, forgive, and celebrate life. It is okay to have fun while striving to be responsible.

Life is full of twists, turns, dead ends, hills, uneven pavement, and mountains. I must listen to my heart and think before reacting. It is imperative to understand words truly hurt as a one-second response can cause a lifetime of pain. We have shortcomings, and sin is sin with different outcomes. Yes, one person may lie and the other may steal, but they are both committing sins in God's eyes. Living and loving in the moment can be extremely rewarding, and of course, sometimes it comes with its challenges. Striving to be honest and kind is important, for we never know who is watching.

I am often told, "You have such a great man by your side." I must agree and realize that this is only because of three letters: GOD! Without God, I do not know where I would be. Life is a struggle at times, but Jai makes me feel like I can do anything. It is extremely important to keep living life and not let cancer take over. We try to do special little things together, like going for a walk, eating out, and of course, shopping. I am sure he can do without the last, but he is such a patient man that he goes and does not complain. I try my best to make him feel special and show him that he is loved and appreciated. I tell him how thankful I am for his commitment and all that he does. He is my rock, and I believe God allowed us to be together to help each other fully grow together into who He has designed us to be. We are much stronger, thanks to our flourishing relationship with God. We focus on each other and what we can do to help the other person feel better. Relationships are about sacrifice. We complement each other as we build on our strengths. Communication is essential, and we discuss our thoughts while sharing feelings about our weaknesses. I must admit, God gave me one special guy. You may see us laughing, joking, smiling, or even crying together. Most importantly, know that we love and trust God for placing us together to serve a higher purpose on this earth.

My journal indicates that today is **August 9, 2014, at 3 am.** I have been unable to sleep for approximately one hour. I had my 5th chemotherapy treatment out of 12 in phase II. It was tolerable, and the Taxol was not as hard on my body. My body has been changing, but for the most part, my weight is remaining the same. I am currently at 166 lbs. I know I should be walking to help with the tiredness. This journey is very emotional at times, but I know God will see my loved ones and me through. We must continue to believe and trust in God.

I feel like the biggest challenge is hair loss, not just from my head but my eyebrows, eyelashes, nose, and more. It is so strange to not have any nose hair! I found out that I needed some hair in my nose to feel it running. I knew that nose hair helps protect the airway from germs and foreign particles, but I did not really think about it restricting expelling fluids. There are days when it takes 30 plus minutes to draw on eyebrows, put eyeliner on, and other makeup to assist with life's "normalcy". I attempt to put makeup on when going places. As Bishop said, we should "look like what we are going to and not what we're going through." I try, and it seems like it makes me feel a little better in the moment. After a few hours, I must admit my head is so hot, I am ready to remove my wig!

My son brings me infinite joy as I go to remove my wig, and he says, "There you are!" He kisses me on my bald head as he gives me a book to read. I can only smile, read to him, and realize we must enjoy every moment of the day.

I had a major sickle cell crisis during the chemotherapy process and had to be placed in the hospital to receive a blood transfusion. The doctors worry about my immune system and health as I struggle with pain, sadness, and just existing. There are days when joy seems so far away, but I continue to pray and believe that it will get better. I stayed in the hospital for a few days, then back to chemotherapy.

Even though I want to stay in bed, I still get up and shower every morning. I look at my physical appearance and notice how my breast size has decreased on one side, scars from surgery under my arm/breast, and countless bruises from bumping my legs and unsuccessful needle sticks. I am a fighter, and I will win this battle. I cannot pretend that it is not difficult, but with love and support, I will continue to grow stronger. God is leading me through this journey, and His path will not allow me to go wrong. His love is beautiful, and I give thanks for the path He has entrusted me to follow.

I am experiencing a range of emotions during this process, but God is right here with me. I am grateful that He continues to trust me with this task even when I doubt myself. There are times when I do not appear appreciative, but I am thankful for all that God does for me and continues to do. I am looking forward to my future and all that He has in store for me. I think about my life and wonder what does God plans to trust me with next?

Sometimes in life, we go through many hardships, and only God knows our true endurance. Psalm 139:13 explains, "For you created my inmost being you knit me together in my mother's womb." God created us, and He knows what we are capable of tolerating and our outcome. I pray that I represent Him well during this journey and help someone along the way, for it is all for God's glory!

It is **September 5, 2014**, and I just made it home from chemotherapy. I have three weeks left! Once chemo ends, I will get a break for a couple of weeks and then start radiation for eight weeks. If all goes well (I am speaking that all WILL go well), I will complete radiation the week before Christmas! What an awesome Christmas present for 2014! To complete chemotherapy and radiation then proceed to have the opportunity to spend the holidays with my family is a fantastic feeling. I am so thankful to God for allowing me to continue to grow stronger as I go through this journey. I had to praise Him as I had an ultrasound and mammogram completed to make sure everything was clear. I can remember finishing the mammogram and ultrasound feeling as if it was Déjà vu. After hearing those "words" from the original test, thoughts always seem to creep back in while I'm waiting on the results. I have learned to speak positivity over myself and trust God when He says it is done!

Today is **February 17, 2015,** and it has truly been an exceptionally long journey! As you probably guessed, I have completed chemotherapy and radiation! Thank God! Chemotherapy was completed on September 26, 2014, and it was a tremendous blessing. I thank God for allowing my mom and aunt to be there for my final treatment. I must admit, my family is beyond the best! It went well, and they were able to access the port without as much difficulty. I think it was due to the thoughts of knowing it was my very last chemotherapy session. Once the medicine was completed, and I was officially "done" with treatment, the nurse said, "You have something else to do." She asked me to stand up and walk with her as it was time to strike the gong! I smiled and proceeded to hit the gong in the treatment room. Other patients applauded and said congratulations. The nurse responded afterward, saying, "You should have hit that very hard." We laughed and agreed it has been a long journey the past few months. She gave me a framed certificate with all the nurses' signatures indicating I had completed chemotherapy.

Going through the process of chemotherapy taught me many important things. It was also a humbling experience showing me how to be grateful for "ALL" things God has granted me. Sometimes, we take the small things for granted, but we must realize that everything we have is due to God's grace and mercy. I would have never thought losing my eyebrows, eyelashes, fingernails, toenails, and hair would cause so much pain. I knew that losing part of my body would be dreadful, but I did not know to what extent. I realized that all these things would be replaced as God allowed them to slowly come back. I noticed eyebrows and eyelashes reappearing, the color/growth of my fingernails and toenails returning, and wounds healing from surgery. I gave God praise for allowing these things to come back, and I soon learned that He was preparing me to lose something that would not return.

I finished radiation on December 10, 2014! Radiation caused my skin to burn, but I knew that those scars would heal eventually. I had been putting medicine on my skin to help with coloration and scarring from radiation. I was told to continue with the medicine, and it should completely heal soon. The radiologist explained this was the last treatment, and they gave me a framed certificate with the signatures from the radiology staff. It was a great day because I was "done" with it all!! I was done with feeling sad, hurting, and crying because I did not "look right." I was done with going to the radiologist five days per week, being sick, and done with the pain of having cancer. It was over, and the holidays were approaching.

I decided to put a small tree up for Christmas since we were going to Mississippi for the holiday. Jesaiah wanted to help with the decorations. Anyone that personally knows me is fully aware that I have a very tiny, not much at all, slight case of undiagnosed OCD. Well, maybe a little more than a slight. I was thinking to myself the ornaments would not be even, and he was just going to put them on there. I agreed he could help, and we started decorating. Whew, did we decorate? It was a small tree, and it was a little scarce, so we needed to organize the ornaments. Jesaiah was not trying to hear it. I made suggestions on where to hang them, but as a 4-year-old boy, he was just hanging them. His words were, "No, Mommy, like this and I'm going to put this one right here."

His father stood in the kitchen laughing because he knew my very tiny, not much at all, slight case of undiagnosed OCD was kicking in. I have worked with children for many years and taught parents not to insensitively correct children when they are young and offering their help. So, I had to let him hang them as I thought to myself that I would go back later to organize them. Okay, I know what you are thinking; it is not a very tiny, not much at all, slight case of undiagnosed OCD. We decorated the tree and had a fun time. He laughed, and he was able to put his ornaments exactly where he wanted them.

It was a couple of days before Christmas. We decided to let Jesaiah open his gifts before we went to Mississippi. We usually take some with us or let him wait until we get back, but we decided to let him open all his gifts beforehand this year. As we sat on the floor, he went to work opening each gift. I think my tiny, not much at all, slight case of undiagnosed OCD had rubbed off on him a little. After opening each present, he would get up and take the wrapping paper to the garbage without being instructed. I handed him a gift, and he replied enthusiastically, "Another one for me, for Jesaiah?" He has such an amazing spirit! He received multiple books and a play dough building set. He wanted to open the play dough, so his father placed cardboard down, and we began to build.

Jesaiah is a highly active child with a creative imagination. There were several colors of play dough, and he wanted to mix them and run them through the machine. I told him we would not be able to separate the colors once they were combined. He said, "It's okay, Mommy," and proceeded. You guessed it, my tiny, not much at all, slight case of undiagnosed OCD was internally saying Nooooooo! It was too late, and since it was his play dough, he mixed it with tons of fun.

It was almost Christmas, so we headed to Houlka, Mississippi to spend Christmas with my family. Of course, Jesaiah wanted to take all his new toys with him and his favorite cars, but we explained he could pick a couple of his new toys to take. He had a handful of his cars, and we got into the "black Nissan car" and turned left. Jesaiah referred to my car as the black Nissan car one evening when I went to pick him up from the babysitter. My car was being serviced, and I had a loaner car from the dealership. When we walked out from the babysitter's house, Jesaiah says "Mommy, where is your black Nissan car? What are you doing in this white

Ford?" So, from then on, we referred to my car as the black Nissan car.

We were in Tupelo, Mississippi (birthplace of Elvis Presley) and headed to my hometown of Houlka (about 20 minutes away). We turned on the Natchez Trace, and Jesaiah immediately says "We're going to see Grandma...We're going to see Grandma!" Even though when we get there, he goes right past grandma to find his cousin, JT. His father says, "Boy, come back and speak to your grandma!" We are in Houlka (the country as we call it) and Jesaiah is in Heaven! He loves going to Mississippi and will often say, "No, Mommy, go this way (turn left from our home), I want to go to Mississippi! I don't want to go see Ms. Tia (turn to the right from our home)." There are few reasons he loves going to the country, but one of his most favorite is the dirt in my mother's yard. Oh, he will spend hours if you allow him, playing in the dirt, by himself. He is perfectly content with running his cars, trucks, and toys through the dirt. The small things in life are the ones that make us so happy. For him, it is Mississippi Dirt!

We had a magnificent Christmas. Jesaiah was able to open gifts and more gifts, so he was incredibly happy. My sister had a big, lovely tree with beautiful decorations (all organized), and he would look under the tree to find his name. We had Christmas lunch/dinner and laughed at Santa (my nephew, Devahn) as he spoke so openly to the children. Jesaiah says, "Devahn, you have on a costume." We all laughed at Jesaiah's observance and freeness to get in pictures. My siblings and I took a group picture, and Jesaiah decided to sit right in this little hole that we left open. It turned out to be siblings and Jesaiah. We continued to take pictures while enjoying moments of exceptional love.

His godparents (Tonya and Johnnie) arrived the next day, and Jesaiah opened their gifts. He received a Lightning McQueen™ Cars™ chair and many educational books. Jesaiah was overly excited to read the books. He sat in his chair reading one of the books they gave him with his legs crossed. He had received a puzzle earlier and asked his godfather to get on the floor to help him put a puzzle together. I told him no as Johnnie had been to church, and he had a suit on. Of course, he did not hesitate to get on the floor to help Jesaiah put the puzzle together. We looked as they sat on the floor together and put a Cars™ puzzle together.

We had a great trip and we headed back to Tennessee. I had a chance to spend time with family and it was a happy time in life! Oh, but God! I had gone through this cancer journey and my life was about to be "normal" again. In actuality, my life would never be normal again. I mentioned earlier that when I turned 33, I thought I would pass away as my brother had. After radiation, I talked to my brother and told him, "Well, I guess what we saw in our visions were signs of your previous step-daughter passing away and my diagnosis of cancer." We agreed and said what a year it had been. We were far from what a year!

I started to think, I was diagnosed with breast cancer on March 28, 2014, and on March 30, 2014, Bishop's sermon was "He Won't Let It Kill You!" That was only the beginning of several messages from God as on that following Sunday in 2014, it was "The Grace to Get Thru It!." Bishop's sermons continued to guide me as he prophetically preached Sunday after Sunday on "Grace Never Gave Up on Me," "Live Through It," "You're Tougher Than That," "Stay There Until,"

"He Can Trust You with It," "I Still Believe" and so much more.

So, God had given me the grace to get through it, and I thought again, what a year! I guess it was all just a coincidence. Oh, but I was wrong. I was far from being through it. God was preparing me for an even bigger testimony with an extremely large test! I have unquestionably learned that the bigger the testimony, the larger the test!

Chapter 7

Philippians 4:13

He Is Good

AS OF <u>DECEMBER 30, 2014</u> (three weeks after finishing radiation), my life would never be the same again. I remember reading a text message at 3:22 pm stating, "Jesaiah was running a fever, so I gave him some Tylenol. He is sleeping right now." My reply at 3:24, "Ok. Thank you! I'm on my way now." I thought about how there were other children there, so I knew I needed to go pick him up. I went to get in my "black Nissan car" and pulled up at the daycare. It was the end of December and very cold.

I got out of my car and knocked on the door. Jesaiah came to the door with his blue puffy jacket on and held his hands up for me to pick him up. I knew then that he was not feeling well. He did not say anything as he laid his head on my shoulder. The daycare worker said he was still sleepy from the medicine she gave him. I thanked her for letting me know and we went to the car. I put him in his car seat to head home.

During the drive, he did not say much of anything the entire way home. He walked into the house and went back to sleep on the sofa. He had been vomiting and did not want anything to eat. His dad arrived and we discussed how he was feeling. He gave him some more medicine and decided to put him in bed. Jesaiah continued to sleep for a few more hours, and then we noticed that he was breathing with his mouth open. We talked about his breathing and agreed we should take him to the children's ER downtown.

When we pulled up and walked into the ER, the waiting room was jam-packed. We waited for a while, and we were checked in around 12 am on **December 31, 2014**. The receptionist asked what was going on, and I explained that he had been running a fever, vomiting, and breathing with his mouth open. She gave me a mask for him and said to step in the room behind her for vitals. The nurse checked his vitals and said they had received a rush of children suddenly. She said he no longer had a fever and gave him some medicine for vomiting. She specified they would give him something to drink later to see if he keeps it down. We were then directed to the corner to register Jesaiah. Afterward, we were told to sit in the waiting area, and someone would be with us. We were eventually called back with two other families.

The nurse placed us in the last room on the observation side. We had never been on that side in all the years we had been going there. His father and I talked about how busy they were and how they admitted him every time we had taken him to the hospital. We waited for at least an hour before the nurse and doctor came into the room. The doctor asked what was going on, and we told her about the fever, vomiting, and mouth breathing. I asked her what would cause him to hold his mouth open while breathing, and she replied, "I am not certain.

The doctor proceeded to say she would swab to check for the flu and complete a chest x-ray for pneumonia. We continued to wait, and they came to get him for the x-ray. His dad walked with them. They returned, and the doctor came back into the room later to report the swab and the x-ray came back clear. She explained that he had an upper respiratory infection and prescribed him some Zofran (even though he had not vomited since being there). They sent us home around 5 am without taking blood or checking for anything else.

We returned home and I worked remotely for a few hours and then went into the office. Jesaiah stayed home with his father, my sister, mom, and aunt. When I returned, he was sleeping on my mom's chest. She said he had been sleeping all day. His dad concurred. Jai explained that for the last hour, he would wake up, scream, and go back to sleep. He placed Jesaiah in the bed, and he started screaming very loudly and went right back to sleep. I said this was not like him. I called the on-call pediatrician and explained what was going on. She asked if they swabbed him for strep or completed any other test on him. I told her no, and she said to take him back to the emergency room. We got him dressed and headed back to the ER. While we were getting him dressed, he was almost lethargic; would not stand up.

When we arrived at the ER, he was lying in his dad's arms. I told them we were just here, and they had sent us home, and now he's just lying in his father's arms. The nurse grabbed him and rushed him back immediately. His room was full of nurses and the doctor. They drew blood, started an IV, and gave him a breathing treatment. They informed us that he did not respond on his right side and that the doctor wanted to complete a CT scan and MRI. While the tests were being performed, the doctor told us Jesaiah had some "concerning things." They wanted to check to see if he had a seizure or stroke as his stats continued to drop into the 70s. During the MRI, they had to stop and give him oxygen. The neurologist explained he had an altered mental status, and his white count was in the 30s.

<u>**On January 1, 2015,**</u> at 1 am, the doctor walked up to me and said, "Your son has bacterial meningitis, and we are heading to critical care." I knew it was serious. My throat began to feel like a knot was in it as thoughts filled my head. Will he be okay? What is going on? We were just here. Now we are going from an observation room to critical care. They provided us with a room so we could rest, and I told his father to go and get some sleep while I stayed in Jesaiah's room.

Jesaiah was hooked up to an intravenous drip and sleeping. I slept in the recliner chair beside Jesaiah and would wake up every time the nurse turned the light on in the room. At 3 am, the doctor came in and woke me up. She said they were going to put a breathing tube down Jesaiah's throat as he was not responding with gag reflexes as expected. She also informed me that she wanted to say this one time to get it over with and would only say it once. I will **NEVER** forget those words. She sat beside me and said, "He could die from this." There was that knot again in my throat and my heart began to race. She went on to say they were going to put electrodes on his head to monitor his brain activity. All the words after, "He could die from this," started to sound like whaa whaa whaa.

I stepped out of the room while they placed a breathing tube down my baby's throat. Everything went so fast and within a few hours, his father returned to the room. He was very emotional as he walked in, and his 4-year-old son was lying in bed with a tube in his throat and head wrapped with a white cloth to secure the electrodes to monitor brain activity. He asked me why I didn't call him. I explained that I did not want to wake him; I felt one of us needed to get some sleep.

When the other doctor came back in, he told us that Jesaiah's ICP numbers were rising, and he needed to place him in a medically induced coma. The doctor declared, "No one could have done anything differently." I knew then, my baby would never be the same. For the next few days, his ICP numbers would continue to rise. They decided to take him off the Phenobarbital medicine to see if he had any brain activity. The monitor did show some, so they placed him back on the sedative. We were surrounded by prayers and knew that God had His hand on Jesaiah.

On Sunday, January 4, 2015, the doctor said his ICP numbers were almost 90 and, on that Monday, the 5th, they dropped to 12. We knew that it was not good, but we were not giving up and told Jesaiah to continue fighting. I leaned down beside my baby, who was wrapped in white cloth and filled with tubes, to give him a kiss. As uncontrollable tears rolled down my face, I whispered in his ear, "Jesaiah… tell God, Uncle Lee, and Bo-Bo, you're not ready and mommy doesn't want you to go."

We were surrounded by family, and we were filling heaven with prayers, promises, and petitions. I had already made God the "promise" when I was a teenager. I recalled my father being in our backyard cleaning fish one summer evening. As my dad cleaned fish, our cousin walked up and shot him multiple times. I prayed, pleaded, and cried to God the entire way to the hospital. Speeding by the trees on the Natchez Trace, I promised God that if He saved my dad, I would do whatever He wanted me to do. I did not make another promise as I had already vowed to do whatever He wanted me to do. I knew that He could save Jesaiah as he had saved my father years ago and as He saved Jesaiah at birth. I filled heaven with tears and prayers to God, asking him to please save my baby.

The doctors took Jesaiah off the Phenobarbital to test brain activity again. To complete the test for brain activity, they would need to measure how much medicine was in his system. They took measurements and sent them off for the test results on January 7, 2015. The doctor explained that the results should return the following day to know how much sedative was still in his body. Elder T. came to pray with us and then called Bishop, who prayed with us between his services. On Thursday, the 8th, the doctor told us the lab did not send off Jesaiah's levels; they were sending them over the weekend. He explained that we could wait if we wanted to, and the results would be in on Sunday, January 11, 2015. His dad and I discussed it and decided to not give up on God or Jesaiah, so we waited until Sunday. While we waited and prayed, our family gathered around us to show support and give love.

As the doctor indicated, the results arrived on January 11, 2015. He informed us that the medicine was out of Jesaiah's body, and they did not see any brain activity. It was complete silence. Sadness immediately consumed the room. He continued to say that he would need to complete two separate exams to conclude if Jesaiah was brain dead. He needed someone in the room with him each time when completing the exams. I did not want to go, so Jesaiah's cousin (Andre) and his father went the first time and then Jesaiah's Uncle Jeremy and my friend Marsha went the second time. Their tears told us all we needed to know. We knew it was not positive without them saying a word.

On January 11, 2015, at 1:16 pm, the doctor pronounced my 4 ½ year old clinically deceased. What does a mom do? How does a happy, joyous child go from playing, hugging, kissing, and smiling to lying in a hospital bed on a ventilator without brain activity?

They asked...*May we share his joy with someone else? Will you harvest Jesaiah's organs?*

His father and I asked each other, what would Jesaiah do? We knew... "Hi, I'm Jesaiah. Nice to meet you!" ...must live on.

We decided to donate his organs, for he was such a happy and loving child. I know he would want someone else to be happy and live on. He would speak to everyone he met, hug strangers, and shake hands while introducing himself. He gave love like none other. I am confident that the people who received his organs are doing the same.

How could I live on after knowing my only biological child had passed when I thought I was supposed to pass away? I was 33. I had not died, but **SUCH** a huge part of me did. I made it through the pain of cancer. Now I must make it through the pain of losing my son.

I knew Jesaiah had passed before the doctor officially pronounced him clinically deceased. The saying goes, "Be careful what you ask God for!" This is absolutely true. I am continuously learning that through God, He will keep our hearts and minds as written in Philippians 4:6-7. I was praying for peace. I asked God to help me and prepare me for His will. On **January 10, 2015, around 7:50 am**, he did exactly what I asked. We were in the sleep room, and Jesaiah's father said he was going to the room to see Saiah while I finished getting dressed. I decided to call my earthly father, and all he said was, "It's God's will" and he loved me. I responded, "Okay, Daddy, I love you too," and we hung up. I thought, Daddy did not say much this morning, but oh he did! I would soon find out that was exactly what he was supposed to say.

Immediately after I hung up, my Pandora app started playing. I said, "That's strange. I didn't turn that on." *Come Fly with Me* by Luther Barnes began to play. It was my first time hearing the song. I listened to the words as I looked out the window. Tears began to fall as if someone was pouring water on my face. I cried out, "My baby is gone."

As the song continued to play, I cried the loudest cry of loss, hurt, and pain as I knew he was not returning. He was in flight home to be with God, my brother, grandfather, and many more amazing angels. I told them to take care of my baby. I heard a voice say, "He's running around playing." Then a sweet angelic sound said, "Mommy, I'm okay." I looked out at the State Capital, and I knew my stinker was truly okay as he flew away to a better place. The lyrics to the song went, *A place where happiness reigns every day, and it's a place where we all can go.*

As I stepped into the shower, I cried and thanked God for the best 4 ½ years of my life. It is like God whispered, *I know you know that Jesaiah's in heaven with me, but I will give you one more confirmation from another father.* I had received affirmation from my earthly father, my Heavenly Father, and I stepped out of the shower to read a text message from Jesaiah's earthly father sent at 8:24 am. "He is good. He is chilling with Many." But God!! Tears started again, and I said thank you, Lord! Ask and you shall receive.

I know that God's grace, mercy, and love surround me daily, for the scripture that I carry very dear to me lets me know "I can do all things through Christ which strengtheneth me" (Philippians 4:13 KJV). He continues to show me, and I can do it but only through Him! My family, friends, and loved ones have been so amazing through all of this. I could not ask for a better support system as I am beyond grateful for everything they have done, are doing, and will do in the future. I pray God's continued blessings upon each of them through this journey called life.

As I looked through pictures of Jesaiah, I decided to write what my baby was able to accomplish in 4 years. God is so amazing, and Jesaiah was one blessed blessing! Jesaiah was able to meet several people and spread joy with his infectious smile and politeness. He spent time with family and friends on holidays, played video games, threw the football, shot basketball, and created beautiful art. He had his own "black Nissan car, and I pack (iPad) while he drove his Lightning McQueen car and motorcycle. He enjoyed reading (initially upside down - the book and/or his body), being in water, and playing on the playground.

He was in a wedding, went to a cabin, rode in a carriage, went to church (loved to sing and clap), and went to the zoo. Jesaiah loved on a sweet dog named Nawlya; even though he was lying in her new doggie bed, she was okay with him. He fed a baby and emptied flour on the floor to run his cars through it (he really loved the dirt). He cracked eggs on the floor, put the shells in the sink (his father does this when he is cooking), and, you guessed it, ran his cars through the eggs!

Jesaiah loved cars. He took several of them apart while completely destroying others. He would take the wheels off the cars but still play with them afterward. He went to birthday parties, and he had a birthday celebration every year with cake. He met Minnie Mouse, the Easter Bunny, Santa, and a princess. He watched racing in person and on television, attended football games, played golf, went fishing, and drove a four-wheeler.

He rode a horse (led by my dad), played in the dirt and sand, stood on a fire truck, wore a college football helmet, put puzzles together, made bracelets, rode trains and horses at carnivals. He danced, wore costumes, and he was able to arrive at his heavenly home in his Lightning McQueen™ casket wearing his Lightning McQueen™ race car outfit and shoes while holding his Lightning McQueen™ car in his hand. Rest in heaven, sweet angel!

"Do nothing out of selfish ambition or vain conceit. Rather, in humility value others above yourselves,"
-Philippians 2:3 NIV

Chapter 8

Life with Exceptional Testimonies

Count It All Joy

THE PAST COUPLE OF MONTHS HAVE BEEN AN EMOTIONAL ROLLERCOASTER. As you are aware, an actual rollercoaster is filled with twists, turns, high points, slopes, and some even take you upside down and in spiral motions. I had moments when I was nauseated, sick, screamed, and even vomited. Of course, there were a few times when I would throw my arms up with a rush of adrenaline and would laugh and cry. When I felt alone on this rollercoaster, I faced fear, distress, and isolation. Life can take you for a ride that is filled with elevation, inversions, slopes, turns, sickness, and excitement. Sometimes rides in life are like steel roller coasters, notorious for a smoother ride but also capable of turning you completely upside down. Then there are wooden roller coasters that are known for airtime in which you are lifted out of your seat. Lastly, there are modern roller coasters that are known for a variety of experiences. For example, floorless, where there is no floor beneath you and your feet are dangling. Then there's the flying coaster, where your feet are strapped in and suspended, and you guessed it... you're standing up. On a rollercoaster, you have a harness, but sometimes in life, it feels like we do not have anything holding us on this ride. It's important to understand that God will protect you and uphold you as He says, "Do not fear, for I am with you; do not be dismayed, for I am your God. I will strengthen you and help you; I will uphold you with my righteous right hand." Isaiah 41:10 NIV

    I know that God will strengthen me as Jesaiah would have been 5 years old on April 16, 2015. This day will always be incredibly special as he lived and celebrated every day. In memory of him, I wanted to "Celebrate4Saiah!" The weekend before, his dad and I decided to go visit his grave in Mississippi. You guessed it; we took him back to MS to the dirt that he loved so dearly! I wanted him placed by one of my other heavenly angels, my oldest brother, Lee. We took him some birthday goodies and put solar lights with balloons attached to his headstone, and we sang happy 5th birthday to him. I wanted to do more as Jesaiah was such a happy kid and loved to do so much. I thought about one of his favorite things to do and decided to share *Jesaiah's Love* with others. My mom came to visit, and she helped me select books off Jesaiah's bookshelf to give to his peers at the daycare. We placed pictures of Jesaiah in every book so that his beautiful smile would be remembered. On his birthday, I went to the daycare and heard, "It's Jesaiah's mom." I could only smile and give them hugs as it brought back memories of when I would arrive, and they would run up and say, "Hi Jesaiah, hi Jesaiah," as they hugged him.

I took the books, along with McQueen bags full of candy, McQueen tattoos, and bubbles, to all the kids. I also gave each child cupcakes, a balloon with either Spider-Man, Mickey Mouse, smiley faces, happy birthday, etc. We had each child write a note to Jesaiah or tell us what they wanted to say. As we attached the notes to their balloons, we noticed that some of the messages read, *I love you, I miss you, I hope you're having fun, I know you're watching me, and Happy Birthday.* We all carried the balloons outside, sang Happy Birthday to Jesaiah, and released the balloons to heaven as we celebrated his 5th birthday.

As we released the balloons at the daycare, his grandmother, cousins, and aunt released balloons and sang happy birthday at his gravesite in Mississippi. This was a bittersweet day as we celebrated the life of my only son. I laughed, cried, and I grieved. We have so many happy memories of a sweet child that God placed here for a season of 4 ½ years.

I am beyond blessed to have such a loving family. I think we often wonder how long our support will be there for us. I do not doubt my family's support, and I am honored while never taking them for granted. They continue to call, text, and send cards to remind me of their love for my beloved son and me. I recently finished "What I Know for Sure" by Oprah Winfrey, and it really made me re-evaluate life and the things I know are certain. For me, God's love, grace, and mercy are definitely factors that are of assurance. He continues to show me love through his everyday blessings. I know some may ask, "How are you able to call yourself blessed after all you have been through?" I am blessed as God gives me deep inner peace on days when life seems upside down. He does not allow me to stray too far away, and He always surrounds me with unconditional love to cherish. We must be grateful as life is uncertain, and it often uses those very excruciating experiences to enlighten us.

It is important to respect and love yourself as it signifies what you demand from others. I have learned that authentic friends encourage you to be better, and they care about you in the good and bad times. When you are down, they are there to elevate you emotionally, spiritually, and/or physically. Never take them for granted and let them know how appreciative you are that they are in your life.

Today is August 16, 2015, and God continues to reveal His plans for my life through His word. I pray, attend church, and God continues to show that He hears me by sending His response through Bishop. It has been this way since I have been attending church here. Many days, I am in complete disbelief. I know when we ask in God's name, if it is God's will, we shall receive. But I must admit, sometimes it is extremely surreal and hard to fathom. I thank God for sending angels and always answering when we think we are not able to move forward.

Bishop's sermon today was *It's Our Time.* and he informed us that "nobody can prevent the plans of God in your life." I know that God has important plans for my life, and he continues to show me through His people. It does not matter how long or how short your life is. You must live! Celebrate moments and enjoy your life! I often hear people say I could make it or do some much better if I had this. God has given us everything we need to "make it," and it is up to us to tap into what we already have. I know that you can make it as God has equipped you with the necessary tools, but you must activate faith and trust in God. Change your saying from *I would like to do this* to *I will do this through Christ, who strengthens me!* Set goals and carry them out for yourself because you want to do them. I decided it was time to write this book because I wanted to help others, and I knew that God would give me the strength to complete it.

So many times, we ask the one-word question, *why*. This is usually after something happens in life, and we begin to ask questions such as: Why did I do it? Why did that happen to me? or Why God? Sometimes we receive an answer almost instantaneously, and other times the response is delayed until the time is right. What if we mentally turned that *Why* into a *Thank you*? I know this is tremendously hard to do while going through a *Why* event.

You may wonder how it is possible to say thank you when a loved one dies, when someone carries an illness or a betrayal from the one who says I love you, or this deep pain/lack that I have. I am not saying it is easy, but when we decide to give thanks during situations, it causes others confusion while we receive a revelation like none other.

When someone or something is confused, it does not know which way to go. In that moment of confusion, God is stepping in and working it out. It may seem like it takes God a while to turn it around but believe me, He is turning it for your good. After God finishes repositioning, you become a survivor, and that could very well be your time to turn your *Why* to *Thank you*.

To give thanks during challenging circumstances, Psalm 55:22 reminds us to "Cast your cares on the Lord and He will sustain you and He will never let the righteous fall." If we show thanks and trust God, He will keep us. It may seem as if we have already fallen or are on the verge of collapsing. When you believe and put actions behind your faith, God will not let you fall completely. I thought several times that I had plunged but realized I was on the verge; I had not fallen entirely. We may stumble and go down to a certain point, but when we trust and ask God, He is able to pick us up before we plummet. Sometimes we receive scars but know that God is there, protecting us as we cast away our cares and believe that he will sustain us through good and bad times. When God sustains us, He sometimes stretches us in the process. How far can one person be stretched without breaking?

It is September 17, 2015, and I feel broken. I cry out to God with hurt, sadness, pain, confusion, loneliness, and weakness. I am pleading with God to show me what He desires of me and help me accomplish it for His glory. I strive to stay above water, but it feels like I just keep slipping under. I know that God is stretching me, and I thank Him for not allowing me to drown in these testimonial tears. Today has been awfully hard as I think about Jesaiah and how much I miss seeing his face, talking to him, hugging, kissing, and just loving on him. He would always give me a hug when I needed it the most. We had so many great moments, and I have continued one of our traditions. It may seem strange to many, but it is my sense of connection. Before Jesaiah passed away, he would come into the bathroom with a handful of cars and sit in front of the shower door while I was in the shower. He would talk to me and play with his cars. The glass shower door would fog up, and I would draw a winding circle on the inside while Jesaiah drew one on the outside. We would laugh as he continued to play with his cars. Once he passed away, I continued drawing the circle on the inside, and I decided to add a fist pound to my big bro and a high five to my grandfather. I knew that these were three of my heavenly angels, and I was always covered. I later added a heart and would write Jesaiah. I continued to do that and still to this day. I questioned why I started drawing a heart. I later found that would be...*Jesaiah's Love.*

    I had to go in for an annual breast MRI and I informed the technician that I was stuck eight, yes, eight times the last time I was here to get an IV for contrast. I explained to the Phlebotomist that the nurse in the lab could get blood with one attempt. He seemed a little nervous and replied, "We're going to give it our best shot." I knew then, I was in trouble. As he prepared the room, I prepared for an IV with deep breaths and prayer. He stuck me twice and said he was going to call for an ultrasound machine. Anxiety set in. I asked why an ultrasound machine. He explained, "With it, I will be able to find your veins and won't have to stick you as much."

    A nurse brought the machine down. He stuck me twice while moving the needle around as he used the ultrasound device. Tears rolled down my face, and I felt flushed with increasing panic because the ultrasound did not work as he said. I told myself to calm down and take deep breaths. I have learned over the years that after the second stick, I'd become anxious. As history has proven, they cannot successfully start an IV or draw blood until several attempts have been made.

The Phlebotomist saw the tears and apologized for sticking me and called the Anesthesiologist.

The Anesthesiologist came in and was very cheerful, saying he was just going to look around. His demeanor was completely different, and I had just prayed again to God, asking Him to please help. He looked at my wrists, hands, and feet. I started praying to God, please do not let him stick me in my foot... please do not let him stick me in my foot, please God. I had it there before, and I knew that was a pain I did not want to go through again. As he continued to search, there was a voice on the intercom saying, please pause for a moment of prayer. I thought, but God!! After the pause, the Anesthesiologist stated he would stick me first with some numbing medicine on the top of my wrist and then start the IV. He successfully started it, and I gave thanks to God and to him.

After the MRI was complete, I was drained emotionally and physically because of the increased stress. I spoke with my sister and told her about my ordeal with the IV needle and multiple sticks. As I was talking to her, sadness overcame me. I thought about the number of times we tell people what hurts, but they do not listen and proceed "their way." Afterwards, they apologized, but the pain could have been avoided if they had listened initially. My sister said I must speak up because I am my best advocate. I explained that I had, but she said I didn't tell him in the "right" tone. We laughed. I told her thanks for talking to me, and we hung up.

God knows exactly what we need and when we need it. When I arrived home and opened my car door, the little 2-year-old boy from the apartment upstairs climbed into my car and gave me a hug. I smiled as I hugged him and thought to myself, thanks, Jesaiah. He was still giving me little hugs when I needed them the most. I walked into the house, looked at Jesaiah's picture, and said I love you so much and miss you beyond words. Tears rolled down my face. I was exhausted. As I stretched out on the sofa, I received a text message, "Hey…are you off? Are you busy? I need my friend." I was at home and not busy, so I prayed for strength and called a friend in need. We talked about her issues, and I told her that I was there if she needed me. I thought now, I would take a nap. God said, not quite as I have one more thing. Jai called to check on me, someone beeped in, but I didn't answer. I told him to hold on, and I checked the message. The voice on the other end said, "This is your doctor. Call me back." I knew then, I was about to be stretched further.

God prepares those who love Him. 1 Corinthians 2:9 (NIV) says, "No eye has seen, no ear has heard, no mind has conceived what God has prepared for those who love him." Sometimes we are unable to understand when God is prepping us, but we must continue to believe and trust in Him. I know that He will continue to guide and see me through as He has already prepared greatness for those who love Him.

I called my doctor back, they placed me on hold while they paged her. When your doctor calls you directly and comes to the phone when you call her back, you know something is going on. She comes to the telephone and straightforwardly says, "Hi Demetris, we reviewed your MRI and found a spot on your sternum. We need for you to come in and complete some additional tests."

There was complete silence as I thought, really, God…another test during this journey. I asked for strength, guidance, and protection as I began to have several scans completed. My doctor ordered a CT and PET scan, but my insurance said they would only pay for the CT scan. They completed the CT scan and could not tell what the lesions were on my sternum, so they had to contact my insurance company again for the PET scan. The nurse called and informed me that the insurance company finally agreed to pay, so I started preparing my heart, mind, and spirit for the exam. I was trusting God and giving Him all the praise. During Sunday service, Bishop said, "God chose you because he knew you could do it." I must be confident and know that God has already worked out what I have not seen, heard, or can conceive.

Many people ask, "How do you do it?" I explain that it is nobody but God. There is no way I could fathom pressing forward without His grace and mercy. I am only here because God decided to keep me and not allow me to drown or completely fall. I cannot pretend that I do not have days when I feel like I am sinking. I must pray, pray, pray, and believe God for protection. Life can be so strenuous, and important to have a strong, loving, and consistent protector to pull us up when we are sinking or falling. No mistake, my family and friends are phenomenal, and I have the mental capacity to realize they have lives. God's strength and love surpass all, and I know I can call on Him at three in the morning, and He is right there. There is no silencing the phone. *I'm sleeping, she'll have to wait, I can't talk right now, or I'll call you back.* God listens right then. He comforts, protects, and provides love to help us through situations. We must be willing to be still and listen to Him while allowing His strength to intercede. Trust and believe as He can protect. I thank God for all those near "drowning" experiences as they have taught me who is there to help pull me up, dry me off, and even resuscitate me. There were times when I almost drowned, but God would not let it be. It has not been an easy journey, but I am surviving while thanking God for his grace, mercy, and numerous rescues and rescuers.

Today is November 5, 2015, and it is 5:30 am. I have been awake since 4:25 am, and my mind has not stopped racing. I'm surrounded by *What if? Will everything be okay?* and *Can I handle this again?* The fear of the unknown can cause heartache and insurmountable stress. I have been praying and believing God's word. Romans 8:28 (NIV) states, "And we know that in all things God works for the good of those who love him, who have been called according to his purpose."

I know that God is present in my life, and I love Him more than words can express. He has shown me many times that His works are for my good. The results may not be what I think is good, but is it what God knows is best for me in this season? His plans for my life are unimaginable, and I must stay focused on his word and love. Am I anxious? Yes. I do worry about what my doctor will tell me today at 10:00 am when she discloses the results of the lesions from the PET scan. Cognitively, I am aware that fear and faith do not "coincide" and realize God has already worked it out. Emotionally, I am nervous as I think about what I have encountered in life and what God may be preparing in His will. Everything I believe is based on God's grace and mercy as I know that He wants me to share His strength, love, and healing with others. I start thinking about my scripture and speaking my ability to do all things through Christ, which strengtheneth me, and I say, Okay Lord, we can handle this! I thank God for always being there and keeping me even when I did not want to keep myself.

My oncologist walks in and says, "I'm going to get straight to it." I feel my heart start beating faster as I have heard this before, but I say, okay, God. She proceeds to inform me, "Demetris, your PET scan did not show anything! Even the spots on your sternum and liver are gone!"

Tears of 'But God' rolled down my face as He continued to confirm His words are true, and we must trust his strength, love, and healing. She hugged me, and I knew that God was right there, keeping me! I am so grateful for God allowing me to have amazing doctors caring for me. I must admit that I would often say, why do all my doctors keep ordering so many tests and scans? I just keep accumulating debt and more debt with all these expensive scans. Now, I say thank you, Lord, for all the earthly angel doctors you have placed around me. I know that the debt is only a small price for my life. I pray for them and ask that He continues to give them wisdom as they extend guidance. They have been there for me, even crying with me, while offering a shoulder to lean on during this journey through life. I am forever thankful for the blessings of my doctors.

"Count it all joy." These past few weeks have been extremely painful as it is the holiday season. I miss my son beyond comprehension, and I am really struggling with being joyous. I am grateful for so many things and especially, God, my family, and friends. Jai and I decided to show thanks. We attended legacy night to honor and celebrate the life of Jesaiah. We quickly learned we are not alone in this journey of trying to count it all joy when you have lost a loved one. The room was full of tears of sadness and heartaches from the loss of beloved children. You could feel the hurt and pain encompassing the place as names of angels were called. It is the holiday season, but our loved ones are not here to celebrate it with us. Christmas is around the corner, and next month marks one year of Jesaiah's return to our Heavenly Father. I strive to be happy during this time, and there are days when depression is knocking at my door. The hurt is unavoidable, but what I know for sure is God's word will help keep my mind, body, and spirit in peace.

As I look at counting it all joy, I realize a few particularly important facts. Without God allowing Jesaiah to grace us with his presence on earth for 4 ½ years, I would not have met some of the remarkable people I have in my life now and I would not know *Jesaiah's Love*. Without counting cancer as joy, I would not know my full strength and that Jai genuinely loves me unconditionally without hair, energy, or the ability to fulfill needs. Without counting Sickle Cell Disease joy, I would not know that I am a survivor who continues to endure. Without counting it ALL joy, I would not have written a book in hopes of encouraging you to count it all joy. I know that it may be extremely hard to look at your situation and relate it to happiness. What you are currently facing or have encountered will, without a doubt, make you stronger. The things I've experienced have been far from happy, but I was able to look back and count them as joyous due to how they contributed to my life. Without God, I would not be able to say these events enhanced my life. I could have easily drowned, but it was not in His plans, and I am forever grateful.

    I know that God hears my prayers as he continues to show me through his word from Bishop and others. It was Sunday and as usual, Jai and I went to eat breakfast after church to discuss the sermon. I told Jai I was really having a tough time during this holiday season. He concurred as we pulled up to the restaurant. We walked in and we were surrounded by Christmas decorations, toys, and music. I went to the restroom and the music was playing in there as well. The music reminded me so much of Jesaiah and I could no longer hold back the tears. I stood over the sink, wiping tears from my eyes with a white paper towel. The more I wiped, the more tears fell. I stepped into the bathroom stall, bent over with tissue in my hand and cried a mother's cry. It was Christmas, and I was broken. As I tried to gain strength, I washed my hands and went to the table where Jai was sitting. I sat down, and the waitress walked up. I told her what I wanted to eat, and as she was taking Jai's order, I stood up and walked back to the restroom. It felt like my heart was full of pain that continued to flow through my tearful eyes. I went back into the stall, and I cried out, "God, please help me, please!" I washed my hands and went back to the table. I sat down, and Jai said, let's have them put it in a box to go.

    I felt broken, hurt, sad, and empty. How could I possibly make it through Christmas without my son? On the following day, God answered. I went to work and interviewed a very spiritual lady. One of the questions pertained to challenges in life. She endured the loss of her son a few years ago and was still coping with it. She informed me that right before she came to the interview, she had picked up two pamphlets and would like to give me one. We walked to her car, and she handed me a pamphlet that read, "Getting through the Holidays when you've lost a loved one." Tears rolled down my face, and she gave me a hug. I asked her how did she know that I was struggling to get through the holidays? She explained that a loss is hard, especially during the anniversary of the death and holidays. I told her about Jesaiah, and she invited me to a group for parents who have experienced the loss of a child. God is so amazing, and I knew that He was helping me at that moment! I pushed through the holidays, and I asked God to have mercy on me.

The past few weeks have been a struggle as <u>January 11, 2016,</u> marked one year since our angel returned to Heaven. I miss him more than words can ever express. I know that he watches from above and smiles down on us often. I have struggled with many things in my life, and I only survived because of God's mercy and grace.

As I was working out, I became overly hot to the point of almost passing out. For the past few years, this has been occurring whenever my body temperature rises. I have consulted numerous doctors before, but no one knows why this keeps happening. I called my current doctor, and she scheduled a cardiologist appointment for that week. The next day, I woke up to a ringing in my right ear. It started to cause my head to severely hurt, and my balance was off. I went to my doctor for them to work me in as I knew something was going on. He examined me and said he was happy that I came in. He explained that I was experiencing Sudden Sensorineural

Hearing Loss and he needed to treat it aggressively. I was speechless. He informed me that I may lose complete hearing in my right ear. The hearing loss was rapidly progressing, and I could not walk without holding on to something. The doctor prescribed medicine for me to start at once and sent me in for more tests as they wanted to look at it further in hopes of my hearing returning in a few weeks.

    I went home to start the medicine and I felt pain in my left knee. I thought, there is no way a crisis is coming on right now. I placed a heating pad on it, took Aleve™, and began to hydrate. I laid there for a couple of hours, and indeed, it was a sickle cell crisis. Within hours, I could not walk by myself, and the pain was so severe that I had to go to the emergency room. They started me on pain medicine and fluids. I began to vomit, and they administered more medicine. They gave me Zofran for nausea and released me with instructions to follow up with my doctor. I called my hematologist, and she told me to come into her office. I was still unable to walk by myself. The pain was not subsiding. The nurse practitioner walked in and at once said, "Let me go get the doctor." My hematologist came in and said, "Take her to the treatment room, start an IV to administer pain medicine, and admit her to the hospital." She did not examine me as she just looked at me and told them to admit me to the hospital. My counts were low, and she said she could not believe they had released me from the emergency room. I knew then it was a serious crisis and asked God again to have mercy on me.

    Everything moved so fast as they started an IV and admitted me into the hospital. I was in pain. They were giving me strong medicine, but I was still awake and hurting. I had been awake most of the night in the ER in constant pain. I received fluids and was placed on oxygen to help increase my breathing. The doctor explained that I was staying overnight, and she would be back tomorrow to see how I was doing. They continued to monitor me throughout the night. The next day, she said my numbers were still low, and they were keeping me on the oxygen, and I remained in the hospital.

I was having a sickle cell crisis. My hearing was almost gone in my right ear. I was in pain but ready to get out of the hospital. I did not want them continuously giving me medicine. Eventually, the pain slowly subsided. I was released a couple of days later and went home to continue resting. As I prayed for healing and restoration, I was better by the end of the week.

We went to church on Sunday and Bishop preached on "The One That Said Thanks." He explained that we should not sit in our situation but pray for a miracle as your breakthrough is tied to your obedience. I began giving thanks to God and letting Him know that I am grateful for all that He does. I praised Him for making me whole inside and out while I prayed for a miracle in my situation. I knew my sickle cell crisis had ceased for the time being, but my hearing loss was still present. I needed God to heal me remarkably as I was striving to be obedient to His word. It is such a challenge to "do right" when you are not feeling your best.

The challenge is even greater when you perceive you are being treated unfairly. I was praying and following God's word, but it felt like I could not catch a break from illnesses. I always give God thanks as I have learned many situations could be a lot worse. I thank him for allowing me to encounter things such as heartache and pain in life. Experiences continue to build my character and transform me into the woman He has designed me to be. I try not to sit in my situation as attacks occur while just sitting there pondering. Negative thoughts, feelings, and assumptions can take over; before I know it, my mind and body will be in full conflict. I believe it is important to give thanks when we do not even feel like it, especially at our lowest. When you can speak positivity in a negative situation, it confuses the adversary. It shows that God is in control, and He will take those things that were meant for your bad and reposition them for your absolute good.

"Do everything in love."
-1 Corinthians 16:14 NIV

Chapter 9

Thriving

Stepping out on Faith

GOD WAS ROTATING IN MY LIFE with exceptional testimonies. It is April 19, 2016, and God has restored my hearing back. I gave Him all the praise. Not only did He restore my hearing back, but He also allowed us to have a blessed day on April 16, 2016. Yes, it was Jesaiah's 6th birthday!!! I know that my baby was celebrating in heaven when we were honoring him on earth. In a large frame on the stage, Jesaiah was wrapped in a white towel, smiling bigger than ever, while words on his picture read, "Of course I would have been there today, but Heaven is just so far away." My heart smiled as we knew that he was present in spirit as six of our earthly angels walked down the aisle to light 6 candles for our heavenly angel's birthday. Photos of Jesaiah were shown on the jumbo screen as Celine Dion's song "Because You Loved Me" played during the candle lighting. His father and I wanted to continue celebrating as we exchanged vows on this incredibly special day.

I looked into his eyes and said, "Baby, as the song declared, God thought I was worth saving. I used to ask why, but now I know why. So that I could experience something that many will not in a lifetime…to be genuinely loved unconditionally and to love the same. Thank you!! I promise to put God first and to pray for you always. You are the most loving and unselfish man that I know. I fell in love with you, and that love continued to grow as I witnessed you with Jesaiah. You gave him your all, and I am so thankful that God allowed you to be his father. I will cherish the memories of our angel above as we go through this journey I call life, with exceptional testimonies. I vow to give you all of me, forever. I'm so blessed that you chose me to share the rest of your life with. Jai, I choose you as my husband, and I promise to love, honor, and be faithful to you for the rest of our lives. I love you always."

After the recessional, we headed outside to a clear, beautiful, blue-skied afternoon. We received red happy birthday balloons, and we released them while shouting, "Happy Birthday, Jesaiah!" We tilted our heads back to look up. Red balloons were floating in the beautiful blue sky for our heavenly angel. This day was made even stronger as we remembered *Jesaiah's Love* while Jai and I united as one. It was a happy and very emotional time. God surrounded us with the everlasting love of family, friends, and special angels. Jesaiah's love was so encompassing that it was contagious. You smiled when he smiled, you hugged when he hugged, you spoke to others when he spoke to others, and you certainly laughed when he laughed. He was exceptional and worthy of continued celebration. His irresistible love was captivating, and it filled your heart with joy. He gave love like none other, with resulted in exceptional testimonies. Our life is forever changed as we remember those tiny arms wrapped around us daily with love and an abundance of happiness.

On May 8, 2016, we attended church in Mississippi. It was a sad time for me as it was Mother's Day. Looking around, I see kids hugging their mothers, giving them roses, and smiles of love. I did not have Jesaiah there to hug me, but I felt the love of family and friends. After service, I walked to the cemetery and placed flowers on my son's grave. He is directly beside my brother (Lee), and I know they are side by side in Heaven.

Some days are extremely hard as I look at pictures of Jesaiah and Lee that are side by side on my dresser. I cry, smile, and rejoice that God allowed these amazing people in my life who taught me so much during their presence on earth: I can do all things through Christ which strengtheneth me, I must not quit when things get hard, give love to others, and celebrate life!

Occasionally, the things and people who we feel are there to help can result in the greatest pain. Just because we think something or someone is meant to help us does not guarantee that it will benefit our total well-being. It is easy to understand that we will experience temporary pain for our gain during some trials and events in life (i.e., exercising). Sometimes the pain is there, and it is causing greater harm than good. I have encountered a situation in which I have had excruciating pain in my ankle, causing me to limp when I walk. I went to my doctor, and she informed me that it has not been injured, but it appears the medicine I am taking to decrease the reoccurrence of cancer is causing joint pain. She explains that joint pain is one of the side effects, but she would like me to continue taking the medicine to see if the pain will decrease over time. I turn to her for clarification and ask, "The medicine that is supposed to help is causing pain, and you want me to continue with it to see if it may stop over time?"

I started to think about this and say to myself, so I am in pain now, and you know what is causing it, but you want me to continue with what's causing it to "see" if the pain stops. How many times in life do we know what is causing our pain, but we continue with it; hope that the pain stops over time? I will admit that I agreed to continue, even though I knew the side effects resulted in hurt and pain. The more I walked, the greater the pain. I prayed and decided the current pain was not worth my wellbeing. I called my oncologist and told her I was experiencing intense pain, and she told me to stop the medicine to see if the pain subsided. I stopped taking the medication, and the pain was ended. There are times when we should seek guidance and wholeheartedly express what we think is best for our well-being.

I thank God for giving me everything I need and even some of the things I desire. I believe what I speak, pray, and work hard for will come to fruition as "I can do all things through Christ which strengtheneth me." God has prepared me for everything that I will and have been through. He comforts me when I am sad and gives me peace during the chaos. God always knows exactly what I need and the time when I should receive it. There are many moments when I feel I need things, but God allows me to see that I'm not on my time but on the time He has designed for me. Through my own experiences, His time is the exact time when I need something. I have been down to what I thought was my very last, but God always provided for me. I have witnessed his grace and mercy through difficult financial, emotional, physical, and spiritual tests. Worrying due to uncertainty causes significant stress and heartache. Remember to trust God wholeheartedly as He is present and will not put more on you than He has equipped you to endure.

There were instances when I said, "Okay, God, I do believe you have mixed me up with one of your other children," as I did not feel like I could withstand it anymore. He reminded me that I was created by Him, and He knows exactly what I can handle. I know that life can be overwhelming and challenging. There may be times when you question yourself and, yes, even God. Sometimes you may have to drop to your knees or just stop in the moment to call on God. Whatever you do, realize God is waiting to strengthen you. Just remember to continuously believe in God and press forward while trusting yourself.

In those moments of adversity, offering God praise shows Him that He can trust us to give Him the glory. Is it always easy? Absolutely not. I believe everyone can praise God in their own special way. Some people choose to praise every night, each morning before they eat, when they get in the car, before they walk into the office, before they walk into their home and after they walk out of their home. Others praise when things are going wrong, and they have tried everything and everyone else, so they go to God as a last resort. If your praise is sincere, I believe God receives the honor regardless. It is important to pray often as it strengthens your relationship with God and helps with deciphering His voice. When asking God for guidance, He can help you achieve the best for your life. He is always there with His loving arms to surround us with comfort and peace. He is just waiting on us. We must trust and believe God will supply needs that are exceedingly above what we ask. When we are tired and unable to sleep, ask God for rest while giving us peace in His arms. There were so many nights that I asked for peace when I was unable to understand the tears. I cried out with unimaginable pain from sickle cells, loss, cancer, and pain from pain. I struggled while praying for strength and comfort. It was eating me up inside. I had to do something about it before it did something about me.

It is November 11, 2016, and it is time to do something about it. As I look in the mirror, it is challenging to truly know the person looking back at me. I continue to make excuses, but it is time to start activating faith and putting actions behind words. I decided to exercise Monday-Saturday in some form to get into a habit of working out and to eat healthier while making a lifelong change. I started this morning with 30 minutes on the stationary bike, and it was not easy as I wanted to stop.

In life, we are sometimes faced with situations that are not easy, and we want to quit. I thought about my brother, Lee. He gave me the reading on "Don't Quit." He always encouraged me to do great things in life and to not settle. I took a moment after exercising to reminisce. Exactly 13 years ago, God decided to take Lee home. I remember the special moments and values he instilled. It is extremely important to embrace every moment as life is uncertain. Life can pull us in many directions, and if we are not cognitively aware, we will lose parts of ourselves during the process. I lost my earthly brother, but I gained a heavenly angel. Life is a balancing act. I pray that God continues to give me stability to remain during this journey.

What can cause hurt when your eyes are shut, your words are silent, and you are in a deep sleep? A love so strong that you think about it during your resting period. For me, that is Jesaiah's Love. I found myself crying out during sleep with tears rolling down my face. I awaken with the gentle words of "it's okay, baby" while Jesaiah's father wraps his arms around me. The grief is so heavy that my heart hurts even during slumber. As the anniversary of his death approaches, I dream about him being in the hospital and lying there all alone. I reach for him, but he does not reach back.

There are still so many questions during this journey of praying for wisdom and strength to maintain. I understand that we all experience seasons filled with challenges, but the pain I feel seems to continue through a season. During this holiday period, people are joyful and happy that it is Christmas. I feel as if I must put on a smile and be cheerful on the outside while crying inside. For many, this is a painful time of the year. Honestly, it can be challenging when others seem so happy and expect you to express cheer.

I am grateful for the birth of Christ. Without His birth, Jesus would not have been able to give His life for us. We celebrate Christ during Christmas, but many who are grieving wonder, what about the birth and life of the loved ones we have lost? I know that Jesus should be the center of the celebration, yet it is often a bittersweet time. When given the opportunity, celebrate your loved ones and take the time to enjoy the life you have been blessed with.

Today marks the day that our lives changed forever, and I remember it like yesterday. It was the last day we saw our 4-year-old walk, talk, and breath on his own. As we prepared to bring in 2015, God was preparing to bring one of His angels home. I thought to myself, well, I guess we will be in the hospital with Jesaiah during the year 2015. Thinking about the saying of whatever you are doing to bring the New Year in, you will be doing it during the new year. Never did I think it would be the last time we would be in the hospital with Jesaiah. Surrounded by family and friends, you could feel the impact of Jesaiah's Love. A little boy's smile, touch, and love that was so strong, it lightened the hearts of many. His love continues to influence others, and I know through prayer, relationships, and wisdom, his memory will impact the world exceedingly, abundantly above all we can ever imagine.

I believe God has great plans to positively impact others. As I prayed today, I thanked Him for the hurt, pain, and sadness of losing Jesaiah. I know this sounds strange to many, but I also know that without the hurt, pain, and sadness, it would not go beyond me. I feel as if the impact is greater than me. It is about you. If I can help you during one of the most painful experiences in life, I know that Jesaiah's Love was for a greater purpose.

We go through situations in life and often gain enrichments, but we often keep those things to ourselves. I am only able to write this book because God helped me to understand that I must share Jesaiah's Love. I pray that you understand wherever you are, whatever you have, or may experience, choose to remain through your pain. Choose to live this life with exceptional tests and let us positively impact lives together, with my love, your love, and Jesaiah's Love.

God has placed outstanding people in our lives to enjoy their presence to the fullest. Everyone plays an important role, but we must choose whether we will embrace them with open arms. Family and friends are important, and some can often become our strength when we are weak. It is hard to acknowledge weakness, and we typically prefer to keep it inside rather than express it. Internalizing pain hurts growth, and it causes damage to the ones who genuinely love us.

Being able to admit and accept help is the first step. I believe we all have something we can improve. When we are blessed to have loved ones who deeply care, it is imperative to embrace them. Sometimes we need encouragement, and other times we just need someone to listen. Family can be one of life's greatest blessings. I am so humbled that God allowed me to be in a family full of love and support. I do not take it lightly as I think family is who God has selected, but it is also anyone who truly provides you with unconditional love. Some of the greatest moments of your life may be with people who are not of the same ancestry, but they are still your family. If you have someone you can trust your hurt, fears, laughter, love, and beliefs with, you have family. Always stay in touch, even if it is just a short "Thinking of you" message. Do not be afraid to genuinely say I love you. You never know what someone may be going through in that moment.

I have experienced many great moments in my life, and I know that I would not be where I am today if I did not have the relationship I have with God. It has flourished through messages I receive from Bishop and other earthly angels while studying His word. I have learned that when you are surrounded by people who love God and acknowledges life's encounters, it helps you to feel loved and accepted despite your challenges.

There were times when I felt down and at my lowest. I would attend church and hear a message from God as if I had gone to Bishop and explained what I was encountering. I must admit, it is beyond a blessing to know that God is listening amid chaos. I am grateful for my church family as they are incredibly supportive and caring. I have attended free grief classes, pre-marital classes, and various sessions on life, health, and love. As I attend church and apply messages, I see my growth toward a better life. Bishop is so anointed, and it is an honor to be in his presence to receive a word from our heavenly father. I love my church family as they embrace the body of Christ and strive to love the community while worshipping in "spirit and truth."

Chapter 10

Missing You

Jesaiah's Love

TODAY IS JANUARY 11, 2017, and it marks two years since the doctor pronounced Jesaiah clinically deceased. We faced several changes on January 11, 2015, as I vividly remember walking to my car surrounded by loved ones but feeling completely alone. We all were hurting, but his dad and I were the two who walked into the hospital with Jesaiah but walked out without him. Life shows us how unforeseen change can occur when we least expect it. We could not avoid the fact that we had lost our 4 ½ year old along this journey.

Change can be particularly challenging and especially difficult when you're dealing with death. We had to prepare to bury our son instead of preparing for our son's 1st day of school. In the end, we had lost our child as he was beginning to start the true adventures of his life. The most challenging change for me has been the absence of Jesaiah's arms around me daily, to hear "love you, mommy." I miss the sound of his voice, laughter, smile, and the amazing love he gave. He was one of the greatest blessings, and I know he was sent for even a bigger blessing. Henceforth today, I will embrace change as I strive to complete the will of God. I know that Jesaiah's love must live on as he was sent for even a bigger blessing. More adventure, new experiences, and incredible memories. Welcome change!

From my experiences, resilience is obtained by enduring change and growth. It can be either rapid or gradual while being a vital part of life. There are many times when it is exciting and new, while other moments can be challenging and fearful. Change does not equal growth. Some change may occur, but we may not grow from it. To grow, we are stretched in various ways. Through tests and triumphs, our strength for expansion is increased. When we must work on expansion, many appreciate the gift of growth more. Our processes may differ, but we encounter situations in development that make us stronger and better able to endure.

I have grown and continue to grow into a strong woman of God. God has shown me what it is like to be stretched by Him. Many of us do not like to be stretched because we are pulled and extended from our natural state. I have learned that when we are comfortable and complacent, God may step in to stretch us for growth. The pulling can hurt; sometimes, we may feel like we are about to break. One thing about God is He will extend us and pull us in the direction for His glory without completely breaking us. So, hold on! It may feel as if you have been broken into pieces but remember it's just God stretching you for growth.

As you know, once something has been stretched, it does not look the same way as before. God will reshape you, and some people may not recognize the "new" you. You will not look like what you have gone through during your stretching process. Your strength, humbleness, peace of mind, and grace will give you exceedingly abundantly more than you can imagine. Always remember Philippians 4:13 as YOU can do ALL things through Christ who strengthens (occasionally stretches) you!

God has great things for your life. I pray that during your season of stretching, you will trust Him not to break you. God's love is our agape love, and Jesaiah's love is your love. Continue surviving this life with exceptional testimonies as we never know what will happen tomorrow. Smile, love, and be kind to one another. Pray, forgive, and celebrate life! **1/15/2017**

We often worry about what do others see when they look at us. I have learned the real question is what God sees when He looks at us. Is your goal in life to please others or to please God by helping others? So often, we are not satisfied with ourselves (internally and externally) and try to fill unhappy voids by gaining affirmation from others. Many people feel they fill voids and fit in by driving a certain car, wearing a particular brand of clothes, living in a specific neighborhood, and associating with people of high status. I can tell you from experience that "things and people" do not fill voids as only God can help you with the feeling of emptiness. Things and people will quit when you need them the most. We must ask God for guidance and when seeking fulfillment and change.

At times, selfish ambition can stand in the way and cause disorder and even greater voids. It is important to have a healthy relationship with God and ask how we can please him versus others. When I honestly do a self-evaluation, I see anger, selfishness, sadness, compassion, integrity, and love. We are not perfect beings. I know that there are many things in life that I must continue to work on. I ask God to show me how I can be more pleasing in His sight. Daily, I ask for forgiveness, grace, and mercy. I know my experiences can help someone in need. I aim to please God by helping others through the word of Christ in the journey of life. I strive to LOVE (Let Others' Views Extinguish) and realize that it can be challenging. It is extremely hard as it affects the way we love ourselves and how people love us. When you genuinely LOVE, you let others' views go, and we look toward God's views. If we could align our internal positive thoughts with our external positive views, we can then LOVE. When you love, look at the heart.

I think we all have exceptional testimonies that are imperative to share. I know that some of our experiences have been saddening while others are joyous. I was on my knees praying on **12/7/2017 at 6 am,** talking to God about Christmas and how hard it is without Jesaiah. He said, "What if Jesaiah sent letters from Heaven?" I continued to pray. Afterwards, I sat on the bed and grabbed my cell phone. I began typing a letter in the notes section **at 6:24 am.** As I talked to God about what Jesaiah would write, it was clear as day. God told me to let others know that Jesaiah loves them, and he misses them. I knew it would not be easy to write the letters, but I felt it would be a way to let loved ones know that Jesaiah was doing okay. I started thinking about the many people who have encountered the loss of loved ones and how they do not receive "closure." I thought this would be a way to further share Jesaiah's Love and help many people express their feelings openly. As you read the letter and some of the exceptional testimonies below, I challenge you to pray and do the following for a loved one in need of closure.

<u>Monday, December 25, 2017,</u> in Houlka, Mississippi:

"Hey, everyone! If you would turn your phones on vibrate and give me about 10 minutes of your attention without talking or checking your phone. I wanted to do something this year in hopes that it will bless you as we strive to bless others. Thank you so much, sis, for allowing me to do this. Each of you are receiving an envelope (with your name, city, and state listed) and please do not open it yet. Instead, I want to take a moment to say thank you! Thank you for your love and continued support. I'm beyond blessed to have such an outstanding family. I do not take you for granted, and I thank God every day for you. Christmas has been a challenge since 2015. It has been almost three years since God called our angel home. Will you please bow your head as I pray?

Thank you… grace; mercy… Christmas…Jesaiah 4.5 years… help us to love others and treat people with kindness…fill us with humbleness… praise you for family and love…thank you for sending your son for our sins…In Jesus' name, Amen!

Now, please close your eyes and take a deep breath. Envision… you're standing outside of your house, and you're walking up to your mailbox, you're at the mailbox, and you take your right hand and open the mailbox. You reach in and pull out the envelope in your hand. Please slowly open your eyes and open your hearts as you open the envelope. Take your time and slowly read the words *(I started playing "I can only Imagine" at a low volume and in a low tone, I said,* **Merry Christmas!!**

Merry Christmas!!!

If I could send you a letter, it would go a little something like this...

Hi, Mr. Tee-Tee Pam!

I miss you!

I miss you hugging me, kissing me, and giving me love!

As you know, mommy is writing a book and I'm so excited! Like many of us, my mommy's time is limited with you, but God has some things he really wants her to do. To complete one of those things, she needs your help with sharing "Jesaiah's Love."

Several people go through life never experiencing true love and kindness from others. You should hear some of the kid's stories here. It's really sad how mean some people are. Oh yeah, you will get to hear them one day as you continue to love yourself and others with unconditional love. I can't wait to wrap my arms around you and give you the biggest hug and smile ever! Until that day, will you please send my mommy a little note about what Jesaiah's Love means to you?

God and I have seen your tears and I want you to know that I'm okay and I'm having a great time. My uncle Lee is keeping me in line (well...sometimes) and my "Pretty Bo-Bo" tells him, let that baby run around! He's amazing! There are so many angels here!!! I have met a lot of family that I did and did not know. They miss you...love youuuu!

I have to go nowww☹...but you know how to reach me. Fall on your knees and call on our Heavenly Father. He always gives me your messages! I miss you, miss you, miss you and I love you so much! There's a song called "I Can Only Imagine" by Tamela Mann (don't tell mommy, but I see her crying when she listens to it). It says can you imagine standing before the King? Guess what? I've already asked him if I could run and give you that big hug and smile at that time!!

As mommy says, "Smile, love, and be kind to one another! Pray, forgive; celebrate life!!"

Love Always,
Your Heavenly Jesaiah

2017

Thank you for reading the letter! While you receive this car (because they were Jesaiah's favorite), please turn to the person beside you and say, **"Can you imagine????"**

Jesaiah loves you guys soooo much and I know that he misses you dearly! Please take this car and know that he thanks you for being in his life. We want to continue sharing his love so please help me by sending a note via text, email, or mail by February 14, 2018…Valentine's Day! I love you guys and God has exceedingly abundantly above more than you can ask or think…just for you!!

Remember, smile…love… and be kind to one another! Pray, forgive, and celebrate life!!!

Now give some of those big Jesaiah smiles and hugs to everyone! Merry Christmas!!!"

Jesaiah's Love

January 3, 2018, from Devahn...Banannnna: "I didn't consider Jesaiah as my cousin. He was more of my little brother. Two words that describe him to me would be fearless and smart. He was very different from other kids. He would watch commercials, and that's how I believe he became so smart. By me traveling all over the World and seeing all the nice places, I know that he's in the #1 Place that I want to go to."

January 6, 2018, from Mr. Tee-Tee Pam: "That bubbliest little bundle that you brought to this family was the most amazing gift you could have ever given your family. You called him Jesaiah. His name literally meant "Salvation of the Lord." He truly was that. Jesaiah and I had so many great memories and choosing one as the most memorable is nowhere fair to the others. Jesaiah never met a stranger, and his personality was huge. When he couldn't even talk, he mouthed the word "IPAD" to me one day in Mississippi when he wanted to play with it. I recall his love for being outside. One day you guys pulled into Mom's yard, he had on the cutest outfit with pure white shorts on; he got out of the car seat and took a new seat right in the mud hole in Mom's driveway. I remember taking Saiah to our old high school and he sat down outside with the janitor who appeared to be in his mid-60s. They began having a conversation as if they were lifelong friends. I just watched for a while in amazement of course. He was so into his "talk" with the janitor, he did not want to leave when I called for him. One of my fondest memories happen to be the week you let me take him to Mississippi. Thank you so much for that. We went shopping, driving, walking through the country, and to the circus. He was potty training that week, and I remember he wanted to go get his granddaddy so we could go to Wal-Mart. Because in his words, "Saiah only wanted to get one toy"; I don't think granddaddy knew it did not have to be a $50.00 toy. Anyway, on the way to granddaddy's house, he said, "Tee Tee Pam, Saiah has to pee." I said can you hold it? Jesaiah replied, "Noooo." So, we pulled over right after the big curve. I put the flashers on, got him out of the car seat; opened the doors so he could pee. He dribbled out 2 drops of pee was said, "Yay!" I laughed so hard. He was very proud of that small accomplishment, which was not small at all to him. He knew he had to get all those little things out of the way because He had plans for Jesaiah that we were not aware of at the time. He was such a good little boy who I never had to spank or yell at, thru all the bags of sugar he poured on grandma's floor or the flour and eggs he put in yours-his love was absolutely PERFECT, and I miss him so much. Those early morning phone calls will be remembered forever...."

January 9, 2018, from Uncle Allan: "Just letting y'all know a remembrance of my little guy, Mr. Energetic. Didn't know how much energy he had until we came up one weekend and he gave me a football. So, I threw it he brought it back over and over. I said, man, he sure does have a lot of energy. Hell, he had me tired. You (his dad) said he's like that all the time. Oh yes, one more thing. Remember, I think it was one Christmas; he had the nerves to ask me, what was my name? He might not have known my name. It's not like he has never seen me before. But what was so funny he said, nice to meet you and he shook my hand and went about his business. That Jesaiah! Never forgot those words. It was my pleasure on meeting you, my guy."

January 12, 2018, from Mr. Grandma: "I have so many memories of Saiah, but I will tell you two of my fondest. He would come in the house and pass right by me, saying, 'Where's JT? Where's JT?' His dad would say, 'Boy, get back here. Speak and give a hug to your grandmamma'. When he was also down here, he would go straight to his sand pile to play. He would come in the house, open the fridge, and stick his little gritty hands in the pickle jar to get him a pickle and give me one. He would eat his and I would eat mine. Later, I finished the jar of pickles...grit and all! I love and miss him so much."

January 12, 2018, from JT: "I remember when we used to play with cars and play in the sand together. I miss you and love you."

January 13, 2018, from Aunt Pearlene: "Jesaiah's love means the world to me. Unconditional love, I gave him every time we met, and he gave it back. The way he would call my name, Aunt Pearleeene, gave me cold chills that felt great and so right. The way he hugged and gave me kisses, then ran away with laughter, made my heart overflow with love. The strength he had, he left with me, and I continue to carry it until this day. That's real love. When he wanted to play outside in the dirt we both, would take our places on the ground. He knew when the small car he was carrying was filled with dirt. What would happen next? We both looked at each other; he would pour the dirt on my head and then, just laugh with joy. Jesaiah, I loved you then and I love you now, can't wait to hear you scream my name, Aunt Pearleeene. When I see you again, I will bring a bald head, a small car of dirt, hugs, and kisses, and no more tears. I Love you."

January 15, 2018, from Mr. Tee-Tee Roshell: "Jesaiah's love means so much to me. Jesaiah's love was selfless and unconditional. He loved everyone. Although he couldn't verbally define love, he was a great example of how we should show love. I missed that message he continuously gave through his actions. Back then, I'd just say, "He's a happy child." Although he was a very happy child, it was more to Saiah's actions. I now get it Saiah. I now always try and show love and regardless of the situation. An unexpected "hey my name is Jesaiah" probably brighten many days. I looked at your picture in Braxton's room and noticed he'd written "miss you" on your picture. We all miss Stinker, as your mom and dad would say. I can't imagine you talking more than you did but I know there will be many exciting stories to tell when we meet again. Jesaiah's love, to me, means loving through actions."

January 15, 2018, from Uncle Travis: "Saiah's love is every time I drink a grape soda, and I have to stop; take it down. Lord knows the one time he drank a grape soda; he didn't choke but just grinned and kept drinking it." (We did not give Jesaiah soda at that time, but when he went to Mississippi, his uncle decided to give him soda and Jesaiah tried to drink it all. I'm sure the grin was "Yes, this is great!")

January 16, 2018, from Braxton: "His love meant the world to me. I always loved what he used to call me and how he always used to cry and smile. He was so energetic and enthusiastic, and it brought joy to my face every time I saw him. He always wanted to get on my back and play horsey because we both used to love doing that. I also loved the fact that he never said my name correctly and never said "Braxton," but it was always "Bason". He will always hold a special place in my heart. I love you guys so much."

January 17, 2018, from Amber: "I never knew how I managed to always be so selfish. I thought life was a long fairytale that I could write as I moved along. Boy, was I wrong? Many things in life I couldn't have planned even if I wanted to, and there are a lot more things I would have never thought would happen to or around me. Love. Agape Love. Jesaiah's Love, that is. A love so innocent. A love so pure. A love so genuine. A love so sweet. I always valued family, and I always knew what a lucky girl I was to have such a gigantic family that sometimes I can't even remember everyone's birthdays, last names or middle names, but I knew we were family. Jesaiah's Love taught me to value that a lot more than I did. A lot of things I couldn't change, but the things I could, I did. Your love made me realize that it's not about me. Once I figured that out?!?! It was smooth riding for me. I try my hardest to be there for people I wasn't around so much for. I try to be a light in everyone's life so no one can say while I'm around, it's been a horrible time. I try to be more relevant in the lives of those who make even the smallest impact on my life. Jesaiah's Love opened my eyes to what I knew all along but never paid attention to. It's hard. Life is hard. Love is hard. Trust is hard. Jesaiah's Love means to me that there are second chances, that there are moments in life that'll take your breath away, but it's not about how long it's away. It's about how you recover and that no matter what you feel, Love should always be in the mix. Unforgettable, uncontrollable and undying love…#JesaiahsLove"

<u>January 19, 2018</u>, from Mr. Tee-Tee Shelia: "When I think of Saiah I think of how we were choosing a name, and little did we know after Dee finalized the name my sister looked in a book and it meant "the one that God saved" immediately we knew he was the blessed one! I loved how his parents taught and implemented for him to be respectful (mostly Jai as Saiah would plead 'noooo Tee-Tee, don't call daddy, call mommy'). I loved how he and I were riding one day, and he said, "umm sir, excuse me, sir," and I'm like, who you talking to? I am a ma'am! He then proceeds in his and James Brown's "man world" by saying, "Mr. Tee-Tee Shelia, please stop by Wal-Mart". My heart melts on how I'd love to

be his guy again with that sweet, brilliant talk. I truly miss that little guy!!"

From Granddaddy: "I miss his grinning self and when he would say 'Hey granddaddy, bye granddaddy'. I miss his smile. He would look up at you and smile; especially when he did something and thought he was going to get away with it."

From Auntie: "I remember him fighting and throwing at JT. When he would come in the house, he would say 'wake up, Auntie, how you feeling?' He would fight me too and I would knock the devil out of him (she and Jesaiah had a fly swatter battle). One time, his daddy put on him the couch and he slipped off it. As long as he did not see his daddy, he was off, but when he thought he heard him walking, boy, he jumped back up on the couch like he was supposed to be."

Dear Shelia,
Today is Friday, March 30, 2018, and you are truly special. You sent a response to Jesaiah's Love! Thank you! A couple of months ago, my computer would not allow me to open the saved document of Jesaiah's Love. I started using it as an excuse and stopped editing the book altogether. My phenomenal husband placed his computer on the table so that I could eliminate the excuse and start back editing the book. But as you can imagine, the devil started interceding with "You know you will not have time to publish it by Jesaiah's birthday." Tears filled my eyes as I promised myself that I

would celebrate Jesaiah every year in a special way and 2018 would be evident by releasing a book in honor of him. I cried out, "God, what am I going to do?" His birthday is less than a month away and the book is not ready. My mind was wondering, and I was panicking. Subconsciously knowing, "God had already worked out what I was trying to figure out."

I walked into the bedroom and grabbed the wooden cross from the bookshelf. In the corner was Jesaiah's chair. I crossed my legs and sat on the floor in front of his chair. While holding the cross in my right hand, I cried out to our heavenly father. Tears upon tears, I asked God to please help me! I was surrounded by little white rolled tissues filled with insurmountable hurt and pain. As I thought about this journey called life, I cried out for guidance, strength, forgiveness, and healing…As I thought about this journey called life, I cried out for guidance, strength, forgiveness, and healing… As I thought about this journey called life, I cried out for guidance, strength, forgiveness, and healing. I began to release some of those things that just would not release me.

Sis, God lifted me up spiritually higher than ever before. I have been lifted but never to this extent. It was the most surreal experience. I was physically on the floor but spiritually no longer there. After thanking God, I opened my eyes to the remarkable words in Jesaiah's chair… "Let the sparks fly." I thought about the song "come fly with me" that started playing when Jesaiah was flying back to heaven on that special morning. Jesaiah used his wings on earth, and I want you to use your wings. Whatever you do in life, fly! My prayer is that you will fly higher than ever before! Know that God has unforeseen blessings for you. We may not always get what "we" want in this journey called, life but never give up. God has great plans for you, so... "Let your sparks fly" and know that Jesaiah's Love is always near!

> Remember to smile, love, and be kind to one another.
> Pray, forgive, and celebrate life.
> #Celebrate4Saiah2018!!

For Jesaiah

Ecclesiastes 12:7 (KJV) - Then shall the dust return to the earth as it was: and the spirit shall return unto God who gave it.

Where will you find him? He has transcended this ray of light, this bundle of joy, pillar of strength, and our Gift from God. Touched by a divine hand, his essence cannot be measured by the number of his days, but by the quality of those days. Hear in the distance his echoes, bowels of laughter, remember that brilliant smile, that could melt the hardest of hearts. The absolute joy he brought to Jai, Demetris, Josh, and all that knew and loved him. How do you measure the length of a life? For Jesaiah it was:

> 4 years, 8 months, 3 weeks, 3 days, 18 hours, and 41 minutes. But the length of days has nothing to do with impact. Ask anyone who ever encountered this beautiful soul how his presence, alone, lit up the room.

A tiny warrior with giant-sized courage who waged and won the battle, long before he arrived here. He came into the world, fully embracing the life he was given and gave it a run for its money. On loan to us, he has returned to the Lord our God, and it is to him that we give praise.

For Jesaiah has left his footprints, as his Aunt Shelia would say, on the Mississippi dirt and on each of our hearts. Full of Life, Light, and Love, and we are all the better for having known and loved him. So, fret not over the length of his days, but rejoice in that he has fulfilled them. I think Dr. King said it best, and I think it's most appropriate here, "like any man, I'd like to live a long and prosperous life, but longevity has its place." So Jesaiah had a purposed life, even though it was not a long life.

To Jai, Demetris, & Josh and to the entire family. May God grant his consolation and strength; encourage you in this night season, raise your hope in the midst of despair. Increase your faith as you struggle to accept His will, comfort you with His peace, and surround you with His unconditional love. And may you always know that God gave you the very best part of Himself when He sent Jesaiah into this world.

I was blessed to both, preview his room and test out his bed during my trip home to D.C. Just before, Jesaiah's anticipated arrival. Dee was all a glow and busy making preparations. His room had all the bells and whistles, and Dee had letters with his name to put on the wall, exclaiming joyfully, " Awe, I don't know where I am going to put them."

At any rate, if I can encourage you any further, it is with this thought that has been my consolation as I think about Jesaiah.

So Jesaiah, you too have a room with a view. He is not lacking anything. He is whole and happy. Heaven is just the right place for him, and his boundless energy will never be contained. I know there will be rough days for you -But his days of struggle have ended, and he is with our Lord.

He is checking out the place that God has prepared for us, and waiting in eager anticipation of the day, when one by one, we will all arrive to meet Jesus- Heaven is a prepared place for a prepared people, and we can't get there anyhow. Will you be ready?

So, if Jesaiah's life should teach us anything, it would be how to number our days, for when the trumpet sounds, we too want to be ready to meet with the Lord and to once again see this gentle and loving soul.

I'll end with this passage....1 Samuel 1:27-28 New King James Version (NKJV)

27 For this child I prayed, and the Lord has granted me my petition which I asked of Him. **28** Therefore I also have lent him to the Lord; as long as he lives, he shall be lent to the Lord." So, they worshiped the Lord there.

Job said, during his greatest losses, The Lord has Given:- and The Lord has taken away, blessed be the name of our Lord.

How lucky he was, Dee, that you prayed him here, just like Hannah, and unselfishly shared him with the world, as you offered him back to God. But he is now resting with the one who sent him, but I know the Joy of having been his mother far outweighs the struggles, suffering, and sacrifice.

And so, today, we again thank God for this undeniable gift.

God Bless You!

Minister ChiQuitta Williams

"For God so loved the world, that he gave his only begotten Son, that whosoever believeth in him should not perish, but have everlasting life." -John 3:16 KJV

Epilogue

Lord, I thank you for your guidance with this assignment on my life. Thank you for helping me to complete it along this journey. Thank you for allowing me to relax and be at peace as I write to help someone who is striving to remain through pain. With You, we shall live to grow.

During hurtful times, try not to embrace unwholesome love. Strive to be mindful of surroundings and be careful about personal space during painful moments. It is imperative to pray for discernment while understanding everyone may not be looking out for your best interest. When seeking God, He will give guidance and direction to help with accepting and forming healthy love. Love that is fulfilling, unselfish, genuine, and honest.

Like many times in life, this started as a journal and ended as a book. We encounter daily events, and we often discuss them with others or write them down. Those daily encounters can lead to the story of our life, reminding us that we must remain even through our pain. The things that are in your journal are contributing to your book. It is up to you to decide if you want to keep journaling or publish a book, keep dating or get married, keep working for others or start your own business; keep love to yourself or share your Jesaiah's Love. How will you choose to make your journal into a book?

"For He guards the course of the just and protects the way of his faithful ones." -Proverbs 2:8 NIV

Love…Always,

Demetris Moore Haney, God's Daughter

"Now unto him, that is able to do exceeding abundantly above all that we ask or think, according to the power that worketh in us…."

-Ephesians 3:20 KJV

Acknowledgments

THANK YOU, GOD, FOR LOVE. Without it, this memoir would not have been possible. I thank every person who shared in JESAIAH'S LOVE as IT IS BIGGER THAN ME; always remember, you can remain through your pain as you are a survivor. You will survive to thrive! Keep loving yourself, others, and God! All glory belongs to Him.

"My mission in life is not merely to survive, but to thrive; and to do so with some passion, some compassion, some humor, and some style." -Maya Angelou

Please visit our surviving to thriving journey at www.thejesaiahfoundation.org

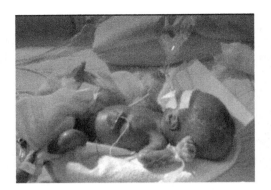

Jesaiah's Love

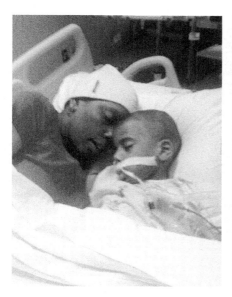
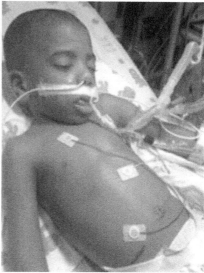

Made in United States
Orlando, FL
13 December 2021